T-34-85
VS
M26 PERSHING
Korea 1950

STEVEN J. ZALOGA

First published in Great Britain in 2010 by Osprey Publishing,
Midland House, West Way, Botley, Oxford, OX2 0PH, UK
44–02 23rd St, Suite 219, Long Island City, NY 11101, USA
E-mail: info@ospreypublishing.com

A CIP catalog record for this book is available from the British Library.

Print ISBN: 978 1 84603 990 4
PDF e-book ISBN: 978 1 84603 991 1

Page layout by: Ken Vail Graphic Design, Cambridge, UK
Index by Alan Thatcher
Typeset in ITC Conduit and Adobe Garamond
Maps by Bounford.com
Originated by PDQ Digital Media Solutions, Suffolk, UK
Printed in China through Bookbuilders

10 11 12 13 14   10 9 8 7 6 5 4 3 2 1

Osprey Publishing is supporting the Woodland Trust, the UK's leading woodland
conservation charity, by funding the dedication of trees.

Author's note

The author would like to thank Stephen "Cookie" Sewell and
Joseph Bermudez for their help in providing archival material on
the North Korean armored force.

CONTENTS

INTRODUCTION

The Korean War (1950–53) presents an intriguing opportunity to compare American and Soviet World War II tanks. These erstwhile allies had developed their tanks in the 1943–44 period to fight German Panzers, only to face one another unexpectedly on a Cold War battlefield. Both the T-34-85 and the M26 Pershing were designed to combat the same foe, the new German Panther tank, which had appeared in action in the summer of 1943. The technical paths taken by the Americans and Soviets were quite different. The T-34-85 was an evolutionary change in the successful T-34 design, substituting a larger turret with an 85mm gun for the earlier smaller turret with its 76mm gun. There was no change in basic tank armor or in other major aspects of the design. As a result, the Soviet Army received its first T-34-85s in early 1944, only about half a year after the program had been initiated. The M26, by contrast, was a fundamentally new design intended to replace the M4 Sherman. Compared to the T-34-85, the US Army's development of the M26 Pershing was quite protracted, the tank not appearing in service until March 1945, more than a year after its program start.

From a purely technical standpoint, a comparison of the T-34-85 against the newer and heavier M26 is not entirely fair. A more approriate comparison would be between the later Soviet T-44 and the M26, which were much closer in their developmental cycles and which were both new designs. Yet the T-44 and M26 Pershing never faced each other in combat, so the point is moot. To add a bit of balance to the comparison, however, this book will more broadly examine the performance of the T-34-85 against all the major types of US medium tanks in Korea, including the M4A3E8, which was closer to the T-34-85 in size and performance.

Korea provides an excellent laboratory for tank warfare, since the major tank-vs.-tank battles were compressed in time to only a few months in the summer and early autumn of 1950. They also took place after the US Army had established a more elaborate operational research effort than had existed in World War II. As a result, there is a great deal of statistical analysis of the tank battles, which helps elucidate the relative performance of the North Korean and American tanks in this conflict.

These studies tended to confirm the results of Allied operational research in World War II. Although military buffs enjoy comparing the purely technical aspects of tank design, such as armor thickness and gun performance, operational research indicates that other factors are far more important in

Snow billows as an M46 of Co. C, US Army 6th Tank Battalion, fires its 90mm gun while supporting the 24th Infantry Division near Song Sil-li, Korea, on January 10, 1952. (NARA)

deciding which side prevails in a tank battle. The simplest condensation of the rule of tank fighting is "see first, engage first, hit first." Research in both World War II and Korea strongly indicated that the side which spotted the enemy force first had a marked advantage. Tanks in a stationary defensive position had an obvious advantage against tanks moving to contact, since the stationary tanks were more likely to spot the approaching enemy first. But regardless of the situation, target acquisition was central to victory in tank fighting.

Do technological advantages such as better armor and better guns affect the balance of tank battles? Korea provides some strong evidence in this debate, since the US side operated several tank types ranging from the M24 light tank and the M4A3E8 medium tank to the larger M26 and M46 tanks. Since crew performance in the US tanks would be similar if not identical, a comparison of the performance of these types in combat helps to provide an answer. The evidence strongly suggests that the newer and more powerful M26 and M46 did have appreciably higher combat effectiveness in the Korean War than the M4A3E8 Sherman.

Yet it is also worth mentioning that the older and lighter M4A3E8 became the preferred US tank in the later phases of the Korean conflict. While this fact may seem to run against the technical performance issue, it is important to point out that the tactical dynamics of the battlefield changed in late 1950. The North Korean People's Army had a sizeable tank force in the summer of 1950, one that had a decisive influence on the battlefield, but the introduction of large numbers of US tanks quickly overwhelmed this force and essentially wiped it out. The Chinese intervention in late 1950 was not accompanied by a significant tank element, and as a result tank-vs.-tank fighting became a rarity in 1951–53. The primary role of US tanks in the later war years was infantry support. While the M26 and M46 still had firepower and armor advantages over the M4A3E8, the smaller tank had mobility and reliability advantages over the newer tank types.

CHRONOLOGY

1943

Summer   Red Army encounters the new German Panther tank, spurring development of an upgunned version of the T-34.

1944

February–May   Forty T25E1 and ten T26E1 prototypes are completed at the Grand Blanc tank arsenal.

March   Soviet Army receives its first T-34-85s.

December   Forty T26E3 tanks are completed.

1945

January   Twenty T26E3s arrive at the port of Antwerp and are assigned to Gen. Omar Bradley's 12th Army Group.

March   T26E3 appears in service and enters action with US forces in Europe. T26E3 is redesignated as the M26 Pershing.

1948

February 8   The North Korean People's Army (NKPA) is formally created.

1949

May   NKPA armored elements are formed into the 105th Armored Brigade.

October   NKPA 105th Armored Brigade receives its full complement of T-34-85 tanks, with each regiment receiving 40 T-34-85 tanks.

1950

June 25   North Korea invades South Korea.

June 27   The NKPA 107th and 109th Tank Regiments meet at Uijongbu, which serves as the staging point for the main attack on Seoul.

June 28   NKPA forces capture Seoul.

July   The USMC mobilizes its 1st Marine Provisional Brigade for deployment to Korea.

July 3   NKPA 109th Tank Regiment takes part in the capture of the port of Inchon.

July 5   The NKPA has first encounter with Task Force Smith near Osan; US infantry unit is attacked by 33 T-34-85 tanks of the 107th Tank Regiment.

July 10   Co. A, 78th Heavy Tank Battalion, suffers defeat at hands of NKPA armor.

July 16   NKPA 107th Tank Regiment moves across the Kum River to support the assault on the surviving elements of the US Army 24th Infantry Division at Taejon.

July 20   Taejon falls to NKPA. US Army and South Korean forces pull back over the Naktong River to the Pusan perimeter.

July 23   NKPA tank assault stopped at Kumchon.

An M26 tank of the Army's 73rd Tank Battalion supports an attack by the 27th Infantry Regiment on August 25, 1950, during the fighting along the Pusan perimeter. (NARA)

August 2	US 8072nd (later 89th) Medium Tank Battalion goes into combat in Korea. Tank units of the 1st Marine Provisional Brigade also begin to arrive in Korea.
August 7	US 70th Tank Battalion arrives on the Pusan perimeter.
August 12	The NKPA 105th Armored Brigade crosses the Naktong River and takes part in attacks on Taegu.
August 17	First US/Republic of Korea (ROK) efforts to break out of the Pusan perimeter, with attacks towards the Naktong River. Battle of Obong-Ni Ridge.
August 27–29	NKPA armored attack down "the Bowling Alley" is stopped by US infantry and Pershing tanks.
September 1	Major NKPA offensive on the Naktong River.
September 16	US landings at Inchon begin.
September 16–20	NKPA 42rd Mechanized Regiment effectively destroyed around Seoul.
September 17	Eighth Army counteroffensive begins breakout from the Pusan pocket.
September 21	Task Force Lynch makes successful offensive to the Naktong-Ni ferry crossing site.
September 26/27	3rd Platoon, Co. C, 70th Tank Battalion, links up with X Corps' 73rd Tank Battalion near Suwon – the first contact between the Pusan perimeter troops and MacArthur's Inchon force.
November	Armor-vs.-armor engagements became increasingly rare from this point until the end of the war.

1951

February	The Chinese People's Volunteer Army (CPV) in Korea is reinforced with four tank regiments.
June	Chinese 3rd Tank Regiment is almost wiped out in fighting with US/UN forces.

T-34-85 number 800, which belonged to the commander of the 16th Armored Brigade, knocked out in the Naktong fighting on September 4, 1950. This newly formed unit, only a few companies in strength, was prematurely committed to the September 1 offensive against the Pusan perimeter, where it was decimated. (NARA)

DESIGN AND DEVELOPMENT

World War II tank development went through three major periods of transformation. The first was the result of tank combat in the Spanish Civil War of 1936–39, which demonstrated that the thinly armored, weakly armed tanks of the 1930s were not adequate when facing enemy 37–45mm anti-tank guns, nor were they suitable for tank-vs.-tank fighting. These lessons led to the fielding of larger and more capable tanks, such as the German PzKpfw III, the workhorse of the Wehrmacht in the *Blitzkrieg* era from 1939 to 1942. They also resulted in the Soviet T-34 tank, which saw its combat debut in the summer of 1941 during the German invasion of Russia.

The T-34 was the premier tank of this generation, and it revolutionized tank design in the opening years of World War II. It established the benchmarks in the "holy trinity" of tank design: armor, firepower, and mobility. The T-34 used thick, well-sloped armor that was invulnerable to frontal attacks from German 37mm and 50mm guns. By contrast, its closest German counterpart, the PzKpfw III, used nearly vertical armor that was far more vulnerable to attack by the T-34. In terms of firepower, the T-34 employed an excellent dual-purpose 76mm gun that was useful for engaging both enemy tanks with armor-piercing (AP) projectiles, and enemy troops and equipment with high-explosive (HE) rounds. The 50mm gun on the PzKpfw III had mediocre anti-armor performance against the T-34 and equally mediocre HE firepower. T-34s also had substantially wider tracks than had been the norm in previous tank designs; these tracks were an essential feature in operations in Russia, where roads were poor and where wet or snowy ground could bog down other tank types.

The unexpected appearance of the radical T-34 design caused the second transformation in World War II tank design. The Wehrmacht responded to the T-34 in a two-step process, first improving the firepower of its existing PzKpfw III and PzKpfw IV tanks as a stop-gap measure, while at the same time initiating the design of an overmatching adversary for the T-34. This new design eventually emerged as the Panther tank in 1943. The Panther raised the bar yet again by introducing even heavier frontal armor and a more powerful gun than the T-34. It saw its combat debut in the battle of Kursk in the summer of 1943 and it set off the third transformation in World War II tank development, one that would result in the design of the principal tanks covered in this book – the Red Army's T-34-85 and the US Army's M4A3E8 and M26 tanks.

T-34-85 DEVELOPMENT

For the Soviets, the appearance of the Panther tank in the summer of 1943, as well as the more widespread use of the new Tiger heavy tank, led to a reconsideration of Red Army tank policy. The disastrous performance of the Soviet tank force in 1941 and 1942 had led to enormous losses in armored vehicles. As a result, in 1942 the Red Army adopted a strict policy to limit changes on the T-34 tank in order to maximize production quantity over quality. A large number of improvements had been proposed since 1941, including the substantially redesigned T-34M with torsion bar suspension, and the T-34-57 with better anti-tank firepower. The only changes that were permitted, however, were relatively minor ones, most often tied to production economies rather than tactical improvements. By the end of 1942, the Soviet main tank directorate was discouraging the development of an upgraded T-34 in favor of manufacturing a substantially more heavily armored version, the T-43, armed with the

A T-34-85 of the 5th Company commander, 2nd Battalion, 16th Armored Brigade, knocked out near Yongsan during the NKPA attempt to overrun the Pusan perimeter in early September 1950. This is an example of a tank produced at Gorkiy Plant No. 112, with the enlarged turret and split vents on the turret roof. Nearly all of the T-34-85s used by the NKPA in the 1950 fighting were from 1945–46 production runs from three Soviet tank plants. (NARA)

same 76mm gun. The appearance of the Panther at the battle of Kursk forced the Red Army to reconsider this policy.

Following Kursk, an assessment by the main Soviet tank research institute compared the combat effectiveness of the T-34 against its German opponents, assigning the baseline value of 1.0 to the current production version of the PzKpfw III. In this assessment, the T-34 rated at only 1.16, the Pzkpfw IV at 1.27, and the Panther at 2.37. While the T-34 had been equivalent or superior to most German armored vehicles on the battlefield in 1942, this was no longer the case by mid-1943. Even the PzKpfw IV had seen significant improvements in armor and firepower, while T-34 improvements had been blocked. The most alarming trend was the increasing thickness of German frontal armor, which was making the Soviet 76mm gun increasingly ineffective in most combat situations.

T-34-85 SPECIFICATIONS

Crew: 5
Combat weight: 32 tonnes (35 tons)
Power-to-weight ratio: 10.5kW (14.2hp)/tonne
Hull length: 6.1m (20ft)
Overall length: 8.1m (26ft 7in)
Width: 3.0m (9ft 10in)
Engine: V-2-34 4-stroke, 12-cylinder diesel, 373kW (500hp) @ 1,800rpm
Transmission: Dry multi-plate clutch, mechanical gearbox, one-stage side drives with side clutches and strap brakes; 4F, 1R gears

Fuel capacity: 545 liters (144 gallons) internal, 270 liters (71 gallons) external
Max speed: 54.8km/h (34.1mph)
Cross-country speed: 30km/h (18.6mph)
Range: 298km (185 miles) on road
Primary armament: ZIS-S-53 85mm gun L/54.6
Max gun range: 13.3km (8.3 miles) for HE indirect fire
Main gun ammunition: 55 rounds
Gun elevation: -5 to +25 degrees
Secondary armament: Hull-mounted and co-axial DTM 7.62mm machine guns

6.1m

As with the Germans in 1941, the Red Army selected a two-step process. While the improved armor of the T-43 was popular, switching to a new design would cut into production. Nor did the T-43 address the armament problem. A straightforward approach would be to substitute a more powerful gun on the existing T-34 as a short-term stop-gap solution, but develop the new T-44 tank, with better armor and a better gun, as a final objective.

There were several contenders for a new gun for the T-34. In 1941, a small batch of "tank-hunter" T-34s had already been re-armed with a tank version of the ZIS-2 57mm anti-tank gun to improve its anti-armor performance. This design was revisited in the spring of 1943, and four T-34s were armed with the 57mm ZIS-4. In mid-August, three of these were dispatched to the front as Special Tank Company 100 under Capt. Volosatov for field trials. The trials were successful enough for the Uralvagon Plant No. 183 in Nizhni-Tagil to create another batch of "tank-hunters" using 170 ZIS-4 guns. In the end, this program was stillborn due to other developments. The main drawback of using the 57mm gun was that its HE round was inferior to that of the existing 76mm gun. The Red Army was well aware that the vast majority of tank targets required the use of high-explosive ammunition, and improving anti-tank performance at the expense of the more versatile HE capability would be foolish.

The alternative solutions were an improved 76mm gun or a new tank created around the existing 85mm anti-aircraft gun. The 76mm S-54 gun was an adaptation of the 3K 76mm Model 1931/38 anti-aircraft gun. With a longer barrel than the existing F-34 76mm tank gun, the S-54 had better anti-tank performance. This performance, however, was not superior enough to warrant its use. Indeed, Soviet tank designers generally disapproved of the German selection of the 75mm KwK 43 on the Panther, feeling that for its size and weight it was inferior to the 88mm gun on the Tiger I. The Soviet designers felt that the 88mm gun offered a better balance of

AP and HE firepower, while the 75mm was optimized for anti-armor performance at the expense of the more commonly used HE round.

Aside from offering versatility in combat, with good anti-armor and HE performance, the Soviet 85mm gun had the added attraction that the ammunition was already in production for the widely used 85mm anti-aircraft gun, as well as its armored-vehicle variants used on the SU-85 tank destroyer and KV-85 tank. The only drawback of this weapon was that the ammunition did not contain as much propellant as ammunition for the 75mm KwK 43 gun, so it offered about 87 percent of the muzzle energy of the Panther gun and correspondingly less penetration. Yet the Red Army recognized the need to balance technical perfection against economic realities, and so accepted the trade-off.

Having selected the 85mm solution, there were two other issues to be settled. Several design bureaus were assigned to a crash program to develop a suitable 85mm gun based on the existing ammunition. One of these resulting designs had to be selected, and there was also some debate regarding how the new gun would be mounted. Some advocated simply mounting it in the existing hexagonal 76mm turret, since this would obviously simplify production. Although the 85mm gun was successfully mounted in this turret, the configuration was extremely cramped and inefficient. By this stage of the war, the Red Army had come to realize that the two-man turret layout of the T-34 was one of the main causes of poor Soviet tactical

A line-up of NKPA T-34-85 tanks, mainly from the 109th Tank Regiment, captured during the fighting in the Naktong bulge in August 1950 and prepared for shipment back to the United States. The tank in the foreground is a typical example of the Nizhni-Tagil Plant No. 183 production, evident from its distinctive turret casting. (NARA)

performance on the battlefield. The tank commander had to split his responsibilities between commanding the tank and serving as the gunner. German tankers found that T-34 units were slow-witted in tank-vs.-tank combat, as the Soviet commanders were distracted from their command responsibilities by having to hunt out targets and threats. While the Soviet 76mm gun had a high rate of fire on paper, in practice the German tankers often found they could fire three rounds for every one fired by their Soviet opponents. The solution to this problem had been addressed in the T-43 turret design by adding a third crewman in the turret as a dedicated gunner, and this solution migrated to the new T-34 variant when the T-43 turret formed the basis for the new 85mm turret. The new turret adopted a larger turret ring to accommodate the heavier recoil of the 85mm gun, and the basic turret armor thickness was also increased compared to the T-34.

In the rush to field an 85mm gun, the Red Army accepted the D5-T gun as a stop-gap in a turret developed at Plant No. 112 in Gorkiy; this was the same gun used in the SU-85 tank destroyer and KV-85 heavy tank. Production began in late 1943. In the meantime, the development of a more refined gun, the S-53, was completed and this became the standard weapon for the T-34-85, entering production in parallel with the D5-T gun at Gorkiy Plant No. 112 in February 1944 and subsequently at Plant No. 183 at Nizhni-Tagil and Plant No. 174 at Omsk in March 1944. The serial production version of the S-53 gun was designated the ZIS-S-53 after its production plant (*Zavod imeni Stalina* No. 92). The T-34-85 Model 1944 with the ZIS-S-53 gun became the standard version and remained in production through 1947. The tanks used in Korea in 1950 were of this type.

The T-34-85 was first deployed with the Red Army in March 1944, and saw its baptism of fire in the battles around Kamenets-Podolskiy on the Ukrainian–Romanian frontier. They were in widespread service by the summer of 1944 during the great Red Army offensive that pushed the Wehrmacht out of the Soviet Union, and continued improvements were introduced through the production run. In August 1944, the turret casting was increased from 75mm (2.95in) to 90mm (3.54in) at the front. In January 1945, an enlarged commander's cupola with a single piece hatch

Soviet T-34-85 production					
Plant	Location	1944	1945	1946	Total
183	Nizhni-Tagil	6,583	7,356	493	**14,432**
112	Gorkiy	3,079	3,255	1,154	**7,488**
174	Omsk	1,000	1,940	1,054	**3,994**
Total		**10,662**	**12,551**	**2,701**	**25,914**

was introduced. Also in early 1945, Plant No. 112 in Gorkiy began manufacturing a widened turret with greater internal volume; the new turret split the ventilator fans and placed one closer to the gun where it was most needed.

The T-34-85 was an adequate stop-gap, since German Panther tank strength was so meager – in May 1944, the Wehrmacht had only 304 Panthers on the entire Eastern Front. T-44 design, however, was underway at the Uralvagon plant in Nizhni-Tagil. The most significant difference between the new tank and the T-34-85 was in the hull (the turrets of both tanks were very similar). The designers wanted to incorporate thicker armor able to resist the 75mm Panther gun without substantially increasing the weight of the tank. The only way to do so was to reduce the hull volume. While the substitution of torsion bar suspension for the bulky Christie spring suspension partially accomplished this goal, another important change was the decision to drop the redundant crewman in the right front hull station, who operated the hull machine gun. This function was not particularly necessary, and the space could be better used to stow ammunition. Prototypes were ready for testing in August 1944, a few months later than the closest American counterpart, the T26E3. The type went into production in late 1944, even though not all of the design problems had been solved. The T-44 represented the culmination of Soviet wartime design efforts, with an impressive mixture of simplicity and high combat effectiveness for a 32-tonne (35-ton) tank. It is interesting to note that the Soviets were able to come very close to the combat capabilities of the German Panther in a design that weighed only about 65 per cent as much. Yet the T-44 never saw combat in World War II, as the first production batches had lingering mechanical problems, and it remained in training units. Production was quite modest by Soviet standards, with only 1,253 being manufactured in 1944–47.

No sooner was the T-44 completed than the Red Army recognized it was a dead-end. The 85mm gun was not adequate to compete against the growing firepower and armor of enemy tanks and an even larger gun was needed. Although the D-10T 100mm gun was tested on both the T-34 and T-44, the only practical solution was to develop an enlarged turret for the T-44, which led to the T-54 tank program in December 1944. Small-scale production of the T-54 began in 1947,

	Sep–Dec 1945	1946	1947	1948	1949	1950	Total
Soviet postwar medium tank production							
T-34-85	3,041	2,701					**5,742**
T-44	335	718	200				**1,253**
T-54			22	593	152	1,007	**1,774**
Total	**3,376**	**3,419**	**222**	**593**	**152**	**1,007**	**8,769**

but the design was not really mature until 1950. The limited production of the T-44 and the slow maturation of the T-54 in the aftermath of World War II meant that none of these more modern types was exported prior the start of the Korean War. The most modern tank sent to allied armies was the T-34-85 and this type would form the basis of the North Korean tank force in 1950. Once T-54 production was well underway in the Soviet Union in the early 1950s, T-34-85 production began in both Poland and Czechoslovakia. However, all the T-34-85 tanks used during the Korean conflict were Soviet-made.

M26 PERSHING DEVELOPMENT

The development of the M26 medium tank by the US Army was also prompted in large measure by the appearance of the Panther, but in a far less direct fashion. US tank development was managed by US Army Ground Forces (AGF), headed by Lt. Gen. Lesley McNair, a brilliant artilleryman who micromanaged most aspects of army organizational development. The AGF's weapons acquisition philosophy was dominated by battle-need and battle-worthiness. Battle-need was the concept that weapons would only be acquired if the troops in the field expressed a clear need for them; McNair wanted to avoid the "mad scientist syndrome," with engineers in the Ordnance Department dreaming up fanciful weapons that would simply clog up the

An M26 Pershing of Co. A, Marine 1st Tank Battalion, moves forward during the fighting to recapture Seoul on September 26, 1950. (NARA)

supply chain without improving the army's battlefield effectiveness. Battle-worthiness was a demand inspired by the army's unhappy experiences in World War I, when many weapons and vehicles manufactured in the United States proved to be unreliable and lacking in combat durability. Of the two requirements, battle-need was the most problematic. It underestimated the tyranny of time, since once the deployed troops demanded a new weapon to meet a pressing need, it would take months if not years to develop the weapon, place it on the production lines, ship it to the field, and train troops in its use. This philosophy was not especially worrisome in more established classes of weapons such as small arms and field artillery, where technological change was less dynamic, but tanks were a relatively new weapon and the pace of technological change in World War II was brisk.

Through the summer of 1943, the US Army had relied on the M4 Sherman medium tank armed with a 75mm gun. While the US forces had encountered the German Tiger I heavy tank in Tunisia, Sicily, and mainland Italy in 1943, the threat initially did not have a major impact on the US Armored Force – Tigers were encountered in small numbers and seldom had a decisive influence on the battlefield. Allied intelligence learned of the appearance of the Panther from attachés in Moscow, and technical details were widely available by the autumn of 1943. In spite of the appearance of this new tank, there was very little reaction in the US Army due to a fundamental intelligence mistake. It was widely presumed that the Panther was simply another German heavy tank like the Tiger I that would be deployed in a limited number of heavy tank battalions at corps or field army level. In fact, it was designed as a medium tank to replace the PzKpfw IV. McNair and the AGF diligently sent teams into the field to inquire whether there was a need for a better tank with a better gun. The last such mission before the Normandy landings, the "New Weapons Board" sent to Italy in early 1944, came back to Washington with little sense of urgency about the need for an improved tank.

In contrast to the US Army's complacency, the British Army was intent on fielding a better gun on its tanks due to the general trend towards increased armor through the war years, and adapted the 17-pdr anti-tank gun to the Sherman turret. The US Army had been experimenting with a 76mm gun in the Sherman since 1942, but there had been little enthusiasm for the design, as it offered only marginally better anti-tank firepower, but inferior HE firepower, than the 75mm gun. In this respect, the US tank commanders echoed the Soviet viewpoint that a tank gun had to have a versatile combination of AP and HE firepower, and not be optimized for only one of the two criteria. The 76mm gun was half-heartedly accepted for production in the autumn of 1943, but at the time of the Normandy landings in June 1944 none were in the hands of combat troops. As a result, when US tank units went ashore on D-Day in June 1944, they were equipped with versions of the M4 Sherman tank little different from the versions in service in November 1943 in Tunisia.

The US Army's Ordnance Department had been working on a follow-on tank for the Sherman since 1942, but with little sense of urgency. The most important innovation in the design was that the transmission was shifted from the front of the tank back to the rear engine compartment. This reconfiguration removed the need for a power-shaft

though the center of the fighting compartment. The power-shaft in the Sherman took up considerable space and led to the Sherman's excessive height, so the new design had a lower, sleeker hull. Yet there was no consensus about what features were important, and the design went through numerous variations as the T20, T22, T23 and T25. These various designs examined different powerplants, different types of suspension, and different armaments. Ordnance favored the T23 design armed with a 76mm gun, but this vehicle was widely criticized by tank officers in the combat theaters, as it used a novel electrical transmission that promised to be a maintenance burden in the field. Even though there was little support from frontline commanders, production of 250 T23 tanks started in November 1943 and lasted through December 1944.

Because of Armored Force views, in May 1943 two more T20 derivatives entered development. The T25 was fitted with 75mm (3in) frontal armor, weighed 33 tonnes (36 tons) and was armed with a 90mm gun. The T26 was essentially similar but with 100mm (4in) frontal armor, and so weighed 36 tonnes (40 tons). The pilots of the T25 and T26 were completed with the controversial electric drive, but recognition of the problems with this technology led to the substitution of mechanical torquematic transmission on the improved T25E1 and T26E1.

Once again, McNair and AGF solicited the advice of forward-deployed tank commanders, but there was little consensus on what type of tank would be needed in the future. With the invasion of France planned for the summer of 1944, the US Army

The M45 105mm assault gun was built in parallel with the normal M26 medium tank. It was essentially similar, but armed with a short-barrel 105mm howitzer. These vehicles were attached to company and battalion headquarters for fire support. Here an M45 of the 6th Tank Battalion fords the Naktong River on September 18, 1950, during the advance out of the Pusan perimeter. The tanks are following a ford marked in the river by an engineer battalion that had surveyed the site earlier. (NARA)

began final steps to prepare its forces for combat in the main European theater. In the autumn of 1943, Lt. Gen. Jacob Devers was commander of US forces in the European Theater of Operations (ETO), a place-holder position until Dwight Eisenhower's appointment at the beginning of 1944. Devers had previously headed the Armored Force and was well aware that US forces had encountered Tigers in Sicily and Italy in 1943. He wanted to make certain that the US Army could better deal with this threat. Devers requested that development of the T26E1 be accelerated and that 250 of these be manufactured as quickly as possible so they could be deployed in the ratio of one per five M4 medium tanks. Ordnance agreed, but also wanted to produce 1,000 of the despised T23 as well. The War Department forwarded these conflicting recommendations to the AGF for review. Lt. Gen. McNair flatly turned down the request on the grounds that there was no demand from troops in the field and that the new Sherman with its 76mm gun was perfectly adequate. Devers continued to press the case for the T26E1 and on December 16, 1943, the War Department issued a

M26 PERSHING SPECIFICATIONS

Crew: 5
Combat weight: 46.2 tons (41.9 tonnes)
Horsepower-to-weight ratio: 10.8hp (8kW)/ton
Overall length: 28ft 4in (8.63m)
Width: 11ft 6in (3.5m)
Height: 9ft 1in (2.77m)
Engine: Ford GAF 500hp (373kW) liquid-cooled, 4-cycle gasoline engine
Transmission: Torquematic with 3F, 1R gears

Fuel capacity: 183 gallons (692 liters)
Max speed: 25mph (40km/h)
Cross-country speed: 20mph (32km/h)
Range: 100 miles (62km) on road
Main gun: M3 90mm gun in M67 mount
Main gun ammo: 70 rounds
Max range: 21,400 yards (19,568m), HE indirect fire
Gun elevation: -10 to +20 degrees

28ft 4in

directive that authorized the production of 250 T26E1 tanks by April 1945. Devers' position was later ratified by Eisenhower, but the T26E1 was far from ready for production, even on a rush basis. A total of 40 T25E1 and ten T26E1 prototypes were completed at the Grand Blanc tank arsenal from February to May 1944.

The army's opinion about the need for new tanks changed abruptly after the Normandy landings in June 1944. Widespread encounters with the Panther in Normandy in June and July 1944 led to an outcry about the Sherman's poor armor and inadequate firepower. The standard 75mm gun on the Sherman was incapable of penetrating the frontal armor of the Panther, and even the new 76mm gun was not up to this task. As a stop-gap, M4A3 Sherman (76mm) production was accelerated, along with the manufacture of new hyper-velocity armor-piercing (HVAP) ammunition, with a tungsten-carbide core. The improved horizontal volute spring suspension (HVSS) was introduced on the M4A3, producing the M4A3E8 version, which entered combat around Christmas 1944 in the Ardennes. This version was the ultimate type of Sherman fielded by the US Army in World War II, and was also used in large numbers in Korea in 1950. In most respects, it is the most direct equivalent of the Soviet T-34-85.

In spite of improvements to the Sherman, clearly a new tank with a much better gun was needed. Trials of the prototype T26E1 tanks in the summer of 1944 were successful enough that on June 15, 1944, the War Department decided that the 1945 tank production program would be changed to permit production of 6,000 T26 tanks. Nevertheless, the testing program uncovered a substantial number of significant modifications that would be needed before series production started. As a result, the series production version with the 90mm gun was designated the T26E3 heavy tank.

In the meantime, a tank-destroyer version of the Sherman tank armed with the 90mm gun, the M36 90mm Gun Motor Carriage (GMC), had already entered production and first saw combat in the ETO in October 1944. The new 90mm gun

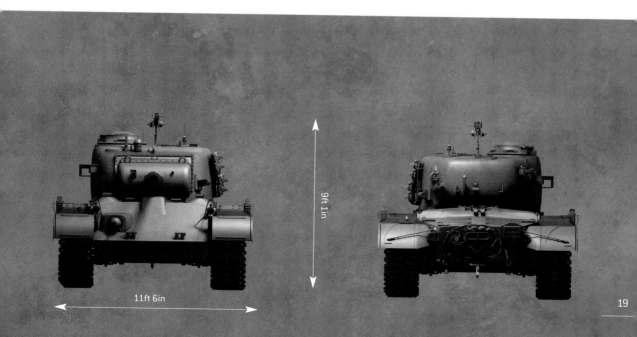

9ft 1in

11ft 6in

had been developed by Ordnance in 1943 for essentially the same reasons as the Soviet 85mm gun: because it could be developed quickly from an existing 90mm anti-aircraft gun. Yet Ordnance showed little enthusiasm for the project due to a lack of corresponding requirement from the field until the summer of 1944, and specialized anti-tank ammunition development was sluggish. When first introduced into combat in October 1944 on the M36, the 90mm gun was still unable to penetrate the Panther's frontal armor at normal combat ranges due to poor ammunition. This situation gradually improved with the advent of HVAP ammunition late in 1944.

By the end of 1944, a total of 40 T26E3 tanks had been completed. There was pressure to do something in response to the growing criticism coming from Europe; the fierce tank fighting in the Ardennes in December 1944 increased the volume of complaints. The head of Ordnance research, Maj. Gen. G. M. Barnes, suggested sending half of the new tanks to Europe for impromptu combat trials – Zebra mission – while the other 20 went to Ft. Knox for the usual tests. The first batch of 20 T26E3s arrived at the port of Antwerp in January 1945 and were assigned to Gen. Omar Bradley's 12th Army Group. They were split into two groups, with ten each going to the 3rd and 9th Armored Divisions. Training for the new tank crews concluded by late February 1945, and the new tanks went into action in March 1945. Those with the 9th Armored Division attracted the most attention when they took part in the capture of the Rhine river bridge at Remagen. Additional batches of T26E3 tanks arrived in late March and early April, and were issued to the 2nd Armored Division (22 tanks), the 5th Armored Division (18 tanks), and the 11th Armored Division (30 tanks). In the final weeks of the war, the T26E3 tanks saw little tank-vs.-tank combat due to the collapse of the German armed forces. By the end of the war, 310 T26E3 had been delivered to Europe of which 200 had been issued to tank units. However, it was only the tanks supplied in February 1945 that saw extensive combat.

The T26E3 experience can best be summed up as "too little, too late." A postwar report by First Army assessed the combat trials of the Zebra mission. "Unfortunately for this test, the German armor had been so crippled as to present a very poor opponent and the cessation of hostilities so soon after forming these companies precluded the gaining of any real experience." In the wake of the war, the T26E3 was standardized as the M26 medium tank. Britain had been naming US Lend-Lease tanks after American generals, such as the "Sherman" for the M4 Series. In 1945, the US Army adopted the British practice and the experimental T26E3 was accepted for service as the M26 Pershing, named in honor of Gen. John "Black Jack" Pershing, who had commanded the American Expeditionary Force in France in World War I. Besides the basic gun version of the M26, the US Army also wanted an assault gun version armed with a 105mm howitzer to provide direct fire support, much as the M4 (105mm) Sherman. This armored vehicle was designed as the T26E2 and accepted for service after the war as the M45.

The June 1944 tank production plan for 1945 called for 7,800 medium tanks consisting of 2,060 T26E3 (90mm), 2,728 T26E2 (105mm howitzer), and 3,000 M4A3 (105mm howitzer). Furthermore, the British wanted 750 T26 (90mm) and 400 T26 (105mm howitzer). By December 1944, in the midst of the Ardennes tank battles, the US Army decided that the T26E2s with 105mm howitzers were less

necessary than the standard 90mm tank version, so the 1945 objective became 4,716 T26E2 (90mm). In point of fact, 2,002 M26 and subsidiary variants were manufactured through August 1945 and only 37 M45 (105mm) howitzer tanks; eventually 185 M45 howitzer tanks were completed. A portion of the M26 fleet was modernized with the M3A1 90mm gun after the war; the gun added a bore evacuator to the barrel to reduce the fumes in the fighting compartment when firing. These were designated the M26A1 Pershing.

The main complaint about the M26 was that its automotive performance was sluggish compared to the M4A3E8 Sherman, since they both were powered by the same engine but the M26 was nearly 9 tonnes (10 tons) heavier. As a result, a program was undertaken after the war to examine better powerplants, and eventually the 552kW (740hp) Continental AV-1790 engine and General Motors CD-850 cross-drive transmission were selected. Construction of ten M46, a modified M26 design with the upgraded elements just mentioned, was authorized in the 1948 budget and 800 in the 1949 budget. The army eventually decided to convert most of its existing inventory of M26 and M45 tanks into the M46 configuration, in addition to new-construction tanks. The plan was to have 810 M46 tanks available by 1950, mainly through conversion, but this schedule slipped. As a result, all four of these tank types, the M26, M26A1, M45 and M46, saw combat service in Korea.

The M46 was a further elaboration of the basic M26 design, but with a new powertrain based on the AV-1790 engine and a new cross-drive transmission. It is most easily distinguished from the M26 by the new mufflers on the rear fenders, as seen in this example of a Marine 1st Tank Battalion M46 re-arming during the fighting in Korea. (NARA)

TECHNICAL SPECIFICATIONS

PROTECTION

The T-34-85 sat between the M4A3E8 and M26 in terms of armor protection. The M4A3E8 was the most weakly protected of the three tanks covered here, both due to the basic armor as well as the armor layout. The T-34-85 actually had thinner front hull armor than the M4A3E8, but more effective protection due to its greater slope; likewise its side armor offered substantially greater protection due to slope rather than thickness. The turret armor of the T-34-85 was also better than on the M4A3E8. In contrast, the M26 offered significantly better frontal protection than the T-34-85, which is not

The US Army in Korea tested the effect of a 3.5in bazooka against the turret of a captured T-34-85, number 212, of the 3rd Company, 1st Battalion, 109th Tank Regiment. The hit on the hull appears to be from tank fire and was probably the cause of this tank's original loss. (MHI)

altogether surprising since it was a later design and a significantly heavier tank. The table on page 24 shows the actual thickness of the major armor surfaces of these tanks, as well as effective thickness, a factor that addresses the angle of the armor. Effective thicknesses are only approximate, since they can vary widely according to the precise angle of shell impact, type of projectile, velocity of projectile, and other factors. The effective thickness figures, therefore, are presented here only to provide a rough comparison.

There were significant differences in armor hardness and tank manufacturing quality between the US and Soviet tanks. The Soviet tank armor tended to be of more erratic quality due to hasty manufacturing by inadequately skilled workers, and it exhibited poor welds by American standards. Soviet tank armor was generally heat-treated to very high hardness (430–500 Brinell) in order to achieve maximum resistance to certain classes of German anti-armor projectiles, even at the expense of structural integrity under ballistic attack. US tank design favored more conventional armor hardnesses (280–320 Brinell) based on US testing. In spite of the sloppy Soviet manufacturing standards, a 1953 report on Soviet ordnance metallurgy warned readers that:

> although welds in Soviet tanks are inferior in quality and much more brittle than corresponding welds in American tanks, this condition has not been a major factor in impairing the battlefield performance of Soviet armor. Poor joint fits, sloppy appearance, jagged and rough finishes should not divert attention from the fact that the Soviet tanks are rugged and battle-worthy and require many fewer man-hours of labor, precision machine tools, jigs, and fixture to construct than corresponding American tanks.

Armor data provides only part of the picture of a tank's protection. Other factors in assessing the vulnerability of a tank include the internal arrangement of fuel and ammunition. The T-34-85 is a clear example of the trade-off between the benefits and drawbacks of steeply angled protective armor. Although the T-34's sloped sides reduced the likelihood of the tank being penetrated by enemy projectiles, it also led to a decrease in internal hull volume. In the event that the T-34 was penetrated, the projectile was far more likely to produce catastrophic damage among the fuel and ammunition stored in such a small space. The side sponsons of the T-34's fighting compartment in particular contained fuel cells that if penetrated could lead to fire and the destruction of the tank. In contrast the US tanks, with their larger internal hull volumes, allowed segregation of the fuel cells in the rear of the tank where they were less likely to be hit and less likely to lead to crew casualties.

Ammunition location poses a significant problem in tank design due to the trade-offs necessary between locating the ammunition away from areas most likely to be hit, while at the same time keeping the ammunition accessible enough to ensure a high tempo of fire. In this respect, the T-34-85's ammunition layout also decreased the

The ammunition stowed in the rear turret bustle made the T-34-85 prone to catastrophic propellant fires that blew off the turret roof. This wreck was inspected by a US Army survey team, which chalked markings on the three visible tank gun hits: one on the turret rear and two against the engine compartment. Judging from the size, they were probably 76mm HVAP projectiles. This particular tank was knocked out during the fighting near the Naktong River in late August 1950. (NARA)

survivability of the tank. The larger size of the 85mm ammunition forced the designers to place a significant portion of the tank's ammo load, 16 of 55 rounds, in the turret, where there was a high probability of being hit. The remainder of the rounds were stowed in the floor or lower hull walls near the loader. The American tanks, however, benefited from US armored combat experiences in 1942–43, which showed the vulnerability of the Sherman to catastrophic damage due to ammunition stowed in the hull sponsons. This situation led to a 1943 program that removed the majority of the ammunition from the sponsons and placed it into lightly armored stowage bins in the floor. This location reduced the likelihood of the ammunition being hit during a penetration, and so also reduced the possibility of devastating tank fires, which were usually caused by ignited ammunition. The lightly armored ammo bins were not well enough protected to prevent penetration by a direct hit, but they were adequate to reduce the vulnerability of the ammunition to ignition by spall or shrapnel from a penetration. The turret bustles on the American tanks were used for radio and machine-gun ammunition stowage rather than main gun ammunition stowage.

The consequences of these design decisions were very evident from combat statistics in Korea. American tanks hit and penetrated by T-34-85 gun fire on average suffered two casualties: one killed and one wounded. This was remarkably similar to World War II casualty statistics. Generally, the crewman in the path of the penetrating enemy projectile was killed and at least one crewmen near the point of entry was injured. If penetrated, a US medium tank was on average likely to incur 42 percent crew

Armor protection comparisons			
	T-34-85	M4A3E8	M26
Glacis thickness	45mm	64mm	100mm
Glacis effective thickness	~122mm	~118mm	~182mm
Hull side thickness	45mm	38mm	50–75mm
Hull side effective thickness	95mm	38mm	50–75mm
Mantlet thickness*	75mm	89mm	115mm
Turret front thickness*	90mm	64mm	102mm
Turret side thickness	75mm	64mm	76mm
Turret side effective thickness	~80mm	~70mm	~80mm

*Effective thicknesses not given for these surfaces since they are curved, and hence variable.

One of the more curious innovations on US Army tanks in Korea in late 1950 was the practice of painting gaudy tiger faces on the front to scare superstitious Chinese troops. Here, an M46 of the 6th Tank Battalion helps extract another M46 from a muddy rice paddy on April 2, 1951, near Chongpyong. These colorful tiger markings remained in use until later in the spring, when they were overpainted during periodic overhaul.

casualties (killed and wounded). About a third of US tanks that experienced a penetrating hit were recovered and put back into action. Yet in the case of the T-34-85 tanks penetrated by US tank gun fire, crew casualties were about double (82 percent) and nearly all were fatalities. Few if any T-34-85 tanks that were holed by US tank guns were recovered, a fact due to both tactical circumstances as well as the tendency of the T-34-85 to suffer an ammunition or fuel fire after penetration.

Aside from NKPA tanks, one of the main threats to US tanks was the 45mm M-42 anti-tank gun; one is seen here after capture by the 5th Cavalry near Waegwan. This was the standard anti-tank weapon in NKPA infantry regiments, which lacked a counterpart to the American bazooka. A total of 550 were in service in 1950. Although the M-42 had limited capability against the frontal armor of the Pershing, it could penetrate the side armor at typical combat ranges. (NARA)

T-34-85 TURRET

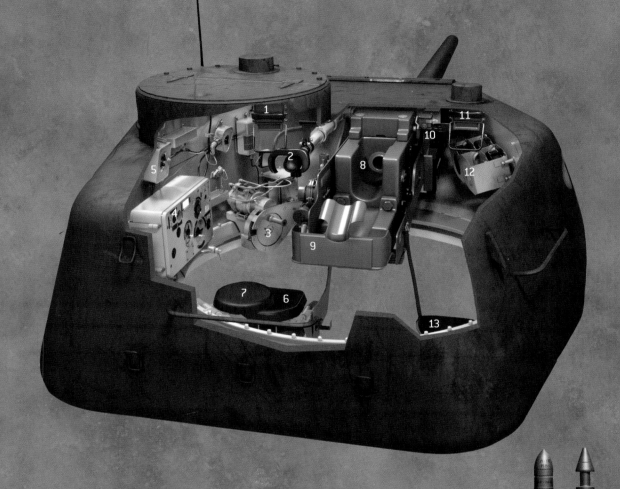

1. Gunner's MK-4 periscope
2. Gunner's telescopic sight
3. Gunner's turret traverse mechanism
4. Tank radio
5. Tank intercom switch box
6. Gunner's seat
7. Commander's seat
8. 85mm gun breech
9. Gun protective cage
10. Co-axial DTM machine gun
11. Loader's MK-4 periscope
12. Ready ammunition rack for co-axial machine gun
13. Loader's seat

UBR-365K AP   UBR-365P HVA

FIREPOWER

In general, the firepower of the T-34-85 was close to that of the 76mm M4A3E8 in terms of anti-armor performance, but superior to the 76mm gun in terms of HE firepower. It was significantly inferior to the 90mm gun of the M26 in AP firepower, and slightly less effective in HE firepower.

The T-34-85 standard ammunition load in Red Army service was 55 rounds, consisting of 36 rounds of HE-fragmentation, five rounds of HVAP, and 14 rounds of AP. In view of the fact that the Republic of Korea Army (ROKA) had no tanks, the North Korean ammo load-out was five rounds of AP and 50 rounds of HE-fragmentation. The precise type of AP ammunition available in 1950 is not known, but at least some HVAP was available (US troops captured some examples). The basic tank-fighting ammunition was the UBR-365 round, which used the streamlined BR-365 AP projectile. In contrast to US AP ammunition in Korea, which had a blunt nose and ballistic cap (the shell was officially known as armor-piercing capped – APC), the BR-365 was streamlined with no ballistic cap. An in-service variation was the UBR-365K, which used the BR-365K with a blunt nose but no ballistic cap. Another difference between US and Soviet AP ammunition was that the latter included a small burster charge inside, which was intended to increase its lethality after penetration; the US projectiles had no charge. The 85mm BR-365 had armor-penetration performance similar to the 76mm M62 round, but it was markedly inferior to the heavier and faster 90mm APC round fired by the M26 Pershing. The most potent anti-armor projectiles available for US and Soviet tanks in Korea were the HVAP rounds, which were composite designs made of light metals such as

The 90mm gun on the M26/M46 family underwent three iterations during production. The final version of the M3A1 used on the M46, as seen here, had the bore evacuator first used on the M26A1, but also introduced a new muzzlebrake. The Marine 1st Tank Battalion was reequipped with M46 tanks after the spring 1951 campaign, to make up for its losses. Here, Co. A rearms for a fire mission on April 25, 1952. By this time, the unit had been moved to western Korea, south of Panmunjom, and was holding a defensive perimeter called the Jamestown Line. The 90mm ammunition was delivered in two-round wooden crates, while the rounds themselves were stored in black fiberboard tubes for added protection. (NARA)

Ammunition employed in tank-vs.-tank fighting in Korea, 1950

	APC	HVAP	HE	WP	Total
M4A3E8	53	43	29	5	**130**
M26	96	35	33	1	**165**
M46	19	16	2	0	**37**
Total	**168**	**94**	**64**	**6**	**332**

aluminum with a heavier and denser tungsten-carbide core. The US assessment of the Soviet BR-365P was that it was based on older German arrowhead ammunition of about 1942 and had a relatively small sub-caliber core. Its performance was inferior to the American 76mm HVAP and markedly inferior to the 90mm HVAP.

The HE ammunition on the T-34-85 reflected Soviet preferences, with the O-365 projectile having a somewhat heavier steel case than comparable US rounds, favoring fragmentation over blast. The Soviet 85mm gun offered a good balance of HE performance and AP performance, while the US 76mm had mediocre HE qualities. Yet the 90mm gun was significantly better than the Soviet 85mm gun in both categories. It was capable of penetrating the frontal armor of the T-34-85 at normal battle ranges; the HVAP ammunition was so powerful that it would sometimes penetrate the front of the T-34-85 and exit out of the rear. The use of various types of ammunition in tank-vs.-tank fighting in Korea was summarized in a US report, shown in the table above. HE and white phosphorous (WP) smoke ammunition was sometimes used after a T-34-85 was hit with AP rounds, in order to kill the escaping crew or to set the tank on fire.

In terms of fire control, the US tanks had a number of advantages. They had two sighting devices linked to the main gun. The first consisted of an M10F periscope in an M73 mount on the roof, with an integral M47A2 telescope. The periscope sight provided the gunner with good situational awareness, since it could be operated at 1x for general surveillance and then switched to 6x magnification,

First-round hit probability in Korean War tank-vs.-tank fighting

Range: yards	0–350	351–750	751–1,150	over 1,150
USA	84 percent	63 percent	39 percent	16 percent
NKPA	50 percent	23 percent	25 percent	0 percent

using the integral telescope for precision aiming. The Pershing also had one of two main telescopic sights fitted. Some used the older M71C with 5x magnification and a 13-degree field of view; others used the newer M83C which offered a variable 4x to 8x magnification.

In contrast, the T-34-85 relied solely on a telescopic sight for aiming. The gunner was provided with an MK-4 periscope, but it was only for general observation, and not linked to the gun for aiming. So after identifying the target in the periscope, the gunner had to then switch to the telescopic sight, with the attendant problems of loss of vital time and the possibility of losing sight of the target. The US sights also offered higher magnification. All three tanks relied on stadiametric rangefinding to compensate for the ballistic fall of the projectile at longer ranges. The US tanks in Korea demonstrated a similar level of first-round accuracy in tank fighting: about 66 percent for the M4A3E8 Sherman and 69 percent for the M26 Pershing. Not surprisingly, first-round accuracy was very dependent on range. Data on North Korean T-34-85 accuracy were much less complete, but were also compiled in a US study, as shown in the table opposite. The average firing range in Korea was about 450 yards (411m).

Besides the observation devices available to the gunner, the commander's sights were also important in fire control, since he was responsible for identifying and selecting the target. In this respect, the US tanks had a decided advantage by offering the commander a more practical cupola better suited to obtaining situational

One of the less satisfactory features of the M26 armament was the placement of the .50-cal. anti-aircraft machine gun on a pintle mount behind the commander's cupola. In order to use it against ground targets, the commander had to exit the tank and fire it from outside while standing on the engine deck. Here, a tanker on an M26A1 Pershing of Co. D, Marine 1st Tank Battalion, takes aim at NKPA troops in the hills near Chochon-dong, during anti-guerilla sweeps there on February 5, 1951.

M26 TURRET

1. M2 .50 cal heavy machine gun
2. 90mm ammunition ready rack
3. Loader's seat
4. 90mm gun breech
5. Gunner's periscopic sight
6. Gunner's telescopic sight
7. Turret hydraulic turret traverse mechanism
8. Gunner's gun control yoke
9. Gunner's turret traverse lever
10. Turret azimuth indicator
11. Gunner's seat
12. Commander's seat

M304 HVAP   M82 APC-T

awareness and target identification. Commanders of both the M4A3E8 and M26 were provided with a vision cupola fitted with six 203mm (8in)-wide view ports, each protected by laminate glass, which gave 360-degree azimuth coverage as well as elevation coverage of -15 to +80 degrees. The T-34-85 commander's cupola was fitted with six smaller prismatic sights that offered a more constricted view of the surroundings. All three tanks also had the periscopic sights noted earlier, fitted to the cupola roof.

The combination of better observation devices and better training meant that US tanks tended to find the North Korean tanks first and engage them first, a critical ingredient in tank duels. Overall, US medium tanks were first to fire in 57 percent of Korean tank duels; in the case of M26 tanks, the figure was 60 percent. According to a US operational research study, by engaging first the US tank units increased their effectiveness in tank duels by a factor of 5.9.

In terms of machine guns, all three tanks had similar armament. Both US tanks had a .30-cal. co-axial machine gun in the turret, and a ball-mounted .30-cal. machine gun in the hull; the T-34-85 likewise had a 7.62mm co-axial machine gun and a hull-mounted 7.62mm machine gun. The main difference in machine-gun armament was that both US tanks were fitted with a .50-cal. heavy machine gun on the turret, ostensibly for anti-aircraft defense. This weapon was very widely used against enemy infantry and unarmored targets such as trucks. The T-34-85 lacked a heavy machine gun.

The T-34-85 enjoyed longer range than the M26 Pershing due to additional external fuel stowage in three 90-liter (24-gallon) drums carried on either side. These were a mixed blessing in combat, for they were vulnerable to small-arms and artillery fire, as can be seen by these punctured drums on a T-34-85 of the 9th Company, 3rd Battalion, 203rd Tank Regiment, 105th Armored Brigade, lost to US forces on July 10, 1950. (NARA)

MOBILITY

In terms of basic automotive performance, the T-34-85 had marginally better speed and range than its American opponents. All three tanks were powered by 373kW (500hp) engines, but the T-34-85 used a diesel engine, while the American tanks were gasoline-powered. As the T-34-85 was lighter, it had a slightly better power-to-weight ratio than the M4A3E8, and a markedly better ratio compared to the M26. The ground-pressure of all three tanks was similar, with the M4A3E8 having the advantage. The T-34-85 carried significantly more fuel compared to the US tanks due to the use of three external 90-liter (24-gallon) fuel tanks and it had significantly longer range.

Firepower comparison

	M4A3E8	T-34-85	M26
Caliber	76mm	85mm	90mm
Type	M1A2	ZIS-S-53	M3
Tube length (calibers)	52.8	54.6	52.5
Tube length	4159mm (163.7in)	4641mm (182.7in)	4718mm (185.7in)
Rate of fire (rpm)	20	3–4	8
Propellant charge weight	2.2kg (4.8lb)	2.9kg (6.4lb)	3.8kg (8.4lb)
Ammunition stowed	71	55	70
Telescopic sight	M71D	TSh-16	M71C or M83C
Sight magnification	5x	4x	5x or 4x and 8x
AP projectile	M62 APC	BR-365 AP-HE*	M82 APC
AP projectile weight	7.0kg (15.4lb)	9.3kg (20.5lb)	10.9kg (24lb)
Muzzle velocity	792m/sec (2,598ft/sec)	792m/sec (2,598ft/sec)	854m/sec (2,802ft/sec)
Armor penetration, @1,000m	109mm (4.3in)	102mm (4.0in)	147mm (5.8in)
HVAP projectile	M93	BR-365P	M304
HVAP projectile weight	4.3kg (9.4lb)	5.0kg (11lb)	7.6kg (16.7lb)
Muzzle velocity	1,036m/sec (3,398ft/sec)	1,030m/sec (3,379ft/sec)	1,020m/sec (3,346ft/sec)
Armor penetration, @1,000m	178mm (7.0in)	130mm (5.1in)	250mm (9.8in)
HE projectile	M42A1	0-365	M71
HE projectile weight	5.8kg (12.8lb)	9.5kg (20.9lb)	10.6kg (23.5lb)
HE projectile HE charge	0.39kg (0.85lb)	0.775kg (1.70lb)	0.952kg (2.09lb)
HE projectile max. range	13.5km (8.38 miles)	13.3km (8.26 miles)	13.4km (8.32 miles)

*Soviet AP projectile is not capped, and has HE bursting charge.

Performance characteristics

	T-34-85	M4A3E8	M26
Weight, combat-loaded	32.2 tonnes (35.5 tons)	33.7 tonnes (37.1 tons)	41.9 tonnes (46.2 tons)
Power	373kW (500hp)	373kW (500hp)	373kW (500hp)
Max. road speed	54.8km/h (34.1mph)	41.8km/h (26mph)	40.2km/h (25mph)
Ground pressure	0.83kg/cm² (11.8psi)	0.77kg/cm² (11.0psi)	0.87kg/cm² (12.5psi)
Fuel capacity	545 + 269 external liters (144 + 71 external gallons)	635 liters (168 gallons)	692 liters (183 gallons)
Road range	298km (185 miles)	62km (100 miles)	62km (100 miles)

Although the T-34-85 had a number of advantages over its American opponents in basic automotive characteristics, it had some significant mechanical shortcomings that undermined its actual performance in the field. The T-34-85 transmission was located in the rear of the tank and was actuated by control rods running under the floor, a system that could prove to be problematic without considerable maintenance. The tank used rough clutch-and-brake steering, and the driver's job was awkward and fatiguing due to the use of spur-gear clash-shift transmission and a multi-disc dry clutch that made shifting difficult as well. T-34-85s had a number of design faults and manufacturing problems that also affected automotive performance. US inspection of T-34-85s captured in Korea found poor soldering of the radiator core fins, a problem that significantly degraded the tank's cooling performance. The single worst fault in T-34-85 engine design was a very deficient air cleaner, which could lead to early engine failure due to dust intake and resultant abrasive wear; several hundred miles of driving in the dusty conditions typical of the Korean summer would lead to severe engine power loss.

Of the two American tank designs, the M4A3E8 was definitely the fleeter of the two, in spite of the M26 Pershing's more sophisticated transmission, simply because they both used the same engine and the M26 was significantly heavier. In the later years of the war, after tank-vs.-tank combat become a rarity, the M4A3E8 was the preferred tank type in Korea due to its better performance in the hill country. The M26 also had a number of automotive teething problems that had not been completely ironed out in 1945, such as weak fan-belts, that could lead to engine overheating. Of the three tank types compared here, the M4A3E8 was the most reliable and durable.

THE COMBATANTS

T-34-85 CREW

The crew of the T-34-85 consisted of five men. In the hull was the driver/mechanic on the left side and a bow machine-gunner on the right side. The turret crew consisted of the gunner in the forward left side and the tank commander behind him; the loader was alone on the right side. The interior of the T-34-85 was very austere; crew

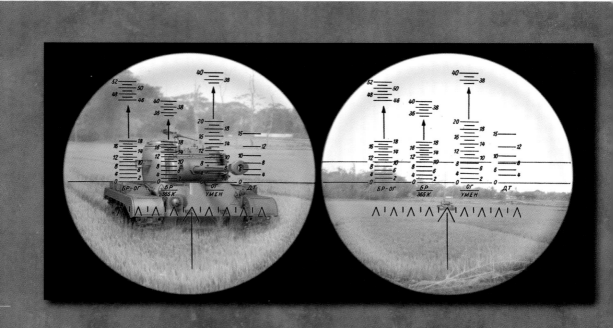

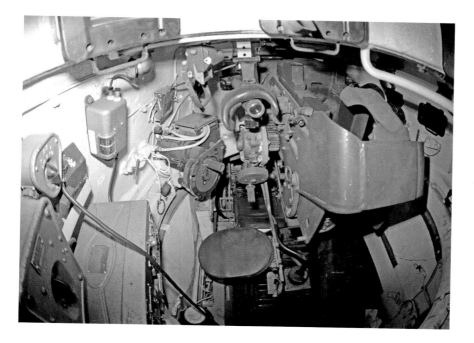

This is the view from the commander's station in the T-34-85 cupola, looking down towards the gunner's station. The TSh-16 telescopic sight can be seen immediately to the left of the protective guard around the ZIS-S-53 85mm gun breech. The tank radio and intercom switch box are evident in the lower left of the photo. (Author)

ergonomics had never been a strong point of Soviet tank design. The T-34-85 lacked a turret basket, and the crew sat on seats suspended from the turret ring. Its interior was considerably more cramped than the M26 Pershing or M4A3E8 Sherman. Ventilation was not especially good in summer weather, and the air became foul very quickly once the main gun began firing. Transit across rough ground was hard on the crew since the suspension lacked any shock absorbers.

T-34-85 GUNNER'S SIGHT

The T-34-85's TSh-16 sight was a 4x power telescope with a simple stadiametric rangefinder configured into the reticle. The four vertical bands are for providing ballistic corrections for the four main types of ammunition (from left to right): armor-piercing (AP), hyper-velocity armor-piercing (HVAP), high-explosive (HE), and the DT machine gun. The lower lines, consisting of upside-down Vs and dashes, provide a stadiametric scale, with the width of the center V roughly equivalent to the length of a tank when viewed at 1,000m (1,090 yards). The horizontal line bisecting the image represents the elevation of the gun. In the view on the left, the gun is at 0 range.

The view through the sight on the left shows the gunner's aim when dealing with a point-blank target, such as encountered during the duel at Obong-Ni Ridge. At a range of under 100m (109 yards), no super-elevation of the gun is necessary as there is essentially no ballistic drop for the projectile.

The view to the right shows an engagement with a Pershing at a range of 1,000m (1,094 yards). In this case, the gunner compensates for the range by adjusting the elevation of the gun upwards, as represented by the horizontal line in the reticle. Since the commander has instructed the crew to use BR-365K HVAP shot, the gunner would adjust the horizontal line to the second set of vertical bands, placing it over the "10" line, which represents 1,000m.

The commander was responsible for directing the rest of the crew. During combat actions, communication was by means of the vehicle intercom via the headsets in the canvas crew helmets. The commander communicated with other tanks in his platoon via the 9RS radio transmitter located on the left turret wall; some tanks had the 12 RDM radio, which was actually intended for self-propelled artillery. During combat actions, the commander would select the target to be engaged, and would direct the gunner while at the same time instructing the loader on the type of ammunition to be used.

The gunner operated the main 85mm gun and co-axial 7.92mm DTM machine gun. When not in action, the gunner could observe the terrain using the MK-4 periscope above and to the left of the telescopic sight; at his left shoulder there was also a small view port, which could be used in conjunction with a pistol port for self-defense. The gunner's position offered very poor visibility of the surrounding environment, and so he depended on instructions from the commander for locating the target. Once a target had been identified, the gunner swung the turret in the intended direction with the electro-mechanical turret traverse, using his left hand. The turret traverse was not precise enough for fine gun-laying, but would move the turret quickly into the rough azimuth, at which point the gunner would do final corrections using the mechanical turret traverse. The gunner elevated and depressed the main gun with the mechanical elevation wheel using his right hand. He aimed the tank's main armament via the TSh-16 telescopic sight and used the stadia in the sight to estimate the range in order to introduce any necessary elevation corrections for either the main gun or co-axial machine gun. The gunner fired by using foot pedal controls, with the left foot pedal triggering the main gun and the right foot triggering the co-axial machine gun. There were also back-up triggers for both weapons.

The loader had a simple seat suspended from leather straps between the turret ring and the gun trunnion. In combat this seat would be folded up out of the way and the loader would stand on the floor. The immediate source of main gun ammunition consisted of a few rounds stowed vertically in the right rear corner of the fighting compartment, and a rack of four ready rounds on the right rear wall of the turret. The turret bustle contained another 12 rounds of ammunition, and there were two more rounds stowed vertically behind the bow machine-gunner. Once all these rounds were expended, the loader would have to extract rounds from the six metal boxes on the floor that contained the rest of the tank's ammo supply. The gunner's job was made more difficult by the lack of an easy or safe means to dispose of spent shell casings.

The driver, as already noted, had one of the most demanding and exhausting tasks of any of the crew due to the relatively simple tractor-style driving controls and the need to activate the rear brakes via mechanical linkages running along the floor to the rear-mounted transmission. To make matters worse, the front driver's station was quite small and cramped, so drivers had to be both short and exceptionally strong to endure the rigors of the job. The driver was also responsible for the maintenance of the engine.

Adjacent to the driver on the right side of the hull was the bow-gunner, who operated the 7.62mm DT machine gun. This position was also relatively cramped and extremely claustrophobic, since the only view of the outside was via the 2x telescopic sight used to aim the machine gun. The lack of a vision cupola in this

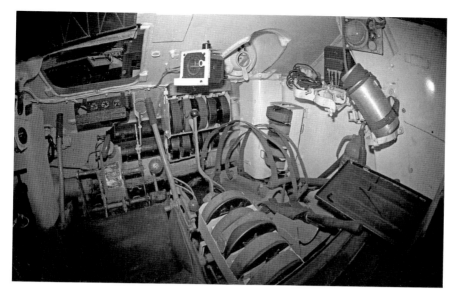

station made it unlikely that the bow-gunner could identify a target unless it was very obvious. The dubious utility of this weapon meant that this position was the first left vacant in the event that the vehicle was undermanned. North Korean People's Army (NKPA) prisoners indicated that this weapon was seldom used, and the co-axial machine gun was the preferred weapon against enemy infantry.

M26 CREW

The crew layout of the M26 Pershing was conventional, like that in the T-34-85, with two men in the hull and three in the turret. One difference was the turret layout, with the tank commander and gunner in the M26 sitting in the right side of the turret rather than the left. In general, the interior of the M26 was significantly more spacious than in the T-34-85, and the configuration much more modern. Korean War tanker memoirs compared the two as "a rudimentary Ford Model T versus a 1945 Cadillac."

The M26 tank commander sat behind the gunner and to the right side of the main gun. He was responsible for directing the tank crew in combat, and also operated the radio, which was located in the bustle behind him. The tank commander had two seats, one at turret race level for riding inside the tank and a folding seat on the turret wall for riding outside the cupola. The "all-vision" cupola had six laminated-glass vision ports, and the hatch had a fitting for either the standard M6 periscope or a 7x periscopic binocular. In contrast to the T-34-85, the commander in the M26 had a remote control for the power turret traverse, which allowed him to swing the turret in the direction of a target to cue the gunner, providing faster reaction time in a tank duel. US tank commanders were issued M7 binoculars, which had a built-in stadiametric rangefinder that the commander used to estimate range. As in the T-34-85, the tank commander

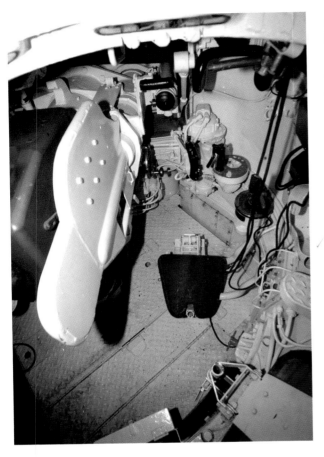

communicated with the rest of the crew via an internal intercom.

The commander also had a .50-cal. heavy machine gun mounted on a pintle behind the cupola. As we have seen, this gun was intended for anti-aircraft defense, but it was used most often for defense against enemy infantry. It was poorly positioned for this role, however, as the commander usually had to exit the tank and stand on the rear engine deck to employ the machine gun for anti-infantry fire. A large percentage of tank commander casualties were the result of this ill-conceived mounting for the machine gun. Although the problem had been well understood at the end of World War II, nothing was done about it in the aftermath of the war.

The gunner sat immediately in front of the commander. He operated the gun elevation manually via a wheel with his left hand. Power traverse was by a joystick at his right hand, and firing could be done either by a trigger on the joystick or by a button on the floor next to his feet. The telescope was the preferred means of aiming the tank armament when engaging precision targets at long range, but the periscopic sight was preferred at close ranges.

The loader sat in the left side of the turret on a small seat that would be folded up in combat, since the loader needed to stand on the turret floor to get enough leverage to move the heavy ammunition. The Pershing had a ready-rack with ten rounds of ammunition stowed vertically in front and to the left of the loader. Once these were expended, the loader would have to extract ammunition from the stowage bins in the floor.

The hull crew consisted of the driver to the left and the assistant driver/bow-gunner to the right. Drivers in the M26 had a considerably easier time than their counterparts

M26 GUNNER'S SIGHT

The M26 gunner could aim the main gun either using the M10F periscope or the M73 telescope. This set of views shows the use of the M10F periscope in order to highlight the value of such a sight. Its main advantage over a telescopic sight was that it provided the gunner with better situational awareness by allowing him to observe the terrain at low (1x) magnification, and then switch to high (6x) magnification for precise aiming. The periscopic sight was generally preferred when dealing with short-range targets or during engagements when rapid response was needed. The telescopic sight was preferred for engaging long-range targets, as it offered better resolution at longer ranges and tended to keep bore-sight better than the periscopic sight, which was knocked out of alignment more easily by vibration or other impacts.

The center lines capped by a "+" sign are the main aiming axis. The horizontal lines provide the necessary ballistic correction for engaging targets at longer range and are gradated in 400-yard intervals. So the "8" represents 800 yards, the "12", 1,200 yards, etc. At a relatively short range of 400 yards, such as seen here, the unitary power view can be used. The view to the right shows the view when switched to higher 6x magnification. Although the reticle here could be used for simple stadiametric rangefinding, US practice was for the tank commander to determine range through binoculars that incorporated a rangefinding reticle. The commander would then instruct the gunner on which target to engage and would provide him with range data at the same time. The gunner would then adjust the horizontal line within the "aiming +" to the proper range.

The turret crew of the M26 Pershing consisted of three men, but there were only two roof hatches, one over the commander's station and one over the loader's. Here is tank B41, the 4th Platoon commander's tank, Co. B, Marine 1st Tank Battalion, seen during a break in the fighting around Inchon on September 19, 1950. The vehicle tactical number in yellow indicates the company, platoon and individual vehicle. The loader is wearing the World War II-pattern tanker's helmet, still standard during the Korean War, and not an especially popular feature due to the lack of comfort and of ballistic protection. (NARA)

in the T-34-85. The Pershing used a more sophisticated torquematic transmission, which was much simpler and less exhausting to operate. Curiously enough, the assistant driver actually did have a set of redundant driving controls on his side of the tank, though there is little evidence that these were widely used. The main role of the assistant driver was to operate the bow gun, a ball-mounted .30-cal. machine gun. The bow-gunner's external vision in the Pershing was significantly better than in the T-34-85, by means of a periscopic sight mounted in the hatch above, though aiming the gun with any precision was difficult. Usually, the gun was aimed by observing the tracer ammunition, but when tracer ammunition was lacking, the gunner would usually aim at the ground and walk the machine-gun fire onto the target.

TRAINING THE NORTH KOREAN ARMORED FORCE

The North Korean armored force began to be formed in 1948 with Chinese and Soviet assistance, following the formal creation of the NKPA on February 8, 1948. A small cadre of North Korean tank personnel was organized in China and trained on captured

Japanese and American tanks, as well as a few Soviet T-34s. The Soviet Army created a special training cadre from officers and NCOs of the Twenty-Fifth Army, which had liberated Korea from the Japanese in 1945. In 1948, the Soviets also formed the 15th Tank Training Regiment at Sadong, in the suburbs of Pyongyang. This unit had two T-34-85 tanks and instruction was provided by a team of about 30 Soviet tank officers. The regiment was commanded by Senior Col. Yu Kyong Su, who had served as a lieutenant in the Soviet Army in World War II and later commanded the North Korean 4th Infantry Regiment. His selection for the command of this important unit was helped by the fact that he was the brother-in-law of premier Kim Il-Sung's wife. The unit's original cadre came mainly from soldiers who had served in Korean infantry units formed since 1945; most of the officers had served earlier in the Soviet or Chinese armies. The initial training consisted primarily of technical instruction, the trainees stripping and reassembling the two T-34-85 training tanks on hand.

In May 1949, the 15th Tank Training Regiment was reorganized and its cadets became the officers of the new 105th Armored Brigade. This formation was intended to serve as the shock force in Kim Il-Sung's invasion of South Korea, so no efforts were spared to prepare it for combat. Since hardly 20 percent of Korean men were literate, recruitment for the tank force was more select than for the infantry.

The brigade was based around the 107th, 109th and 203rd Tank Regiments. It received its full complement of T-34-85 tanks in October 1949, with each regiment receiving 40 T-34-85 tanks. The brigade also included the 308th Armored Battalion with 16 SU-76M assault guns and the truck-mounted 206th Motorized Infantry Regiment. The brigade went through intensive training through the spring of 1950. The training tasks of the former 15th Tank Training Regiment were shifted to the newly formed 208th Tank Training Regiment under the command of Col. Kim Chol Won, a Chinese People's Liberation Army veteran.

The NKPA T-34-85s were almost all from 1945 and 1946 production batches. This particular example is in the Uralvagon Plant No. 183 configuration, evident from the shape of its turret casting.

Besides the T-34-85, the other major NKPA armored vehicle was the SU-76M assault gun. This SU-76M was knocked out along the road to Taegu in the Waegwan sector of the Pusan perimeter during the fighting, on August 20, 1950, with the 27th Regimental Combat Team (RCT), 25th Infantry Division.

One of the main problems facing the Soviet instructors was the shortage of translators. Few Russians had any knowledge of the Korean language, and most of the Korean soldiers who had served in the Red Army in World War II were earmarked for command slots in the NKPA, not for employment as translators. Indeed, many of the higher-level command documents were written in Russian. The brigade never trained to operate as a unified unit; rather, it was intended for use in its component parts for infantry support, with the individual tank regiments attached to infantry divisions in the offensive.

With its full complement of equipment on hand, the component elements of the brigade were dispatched to separate bases for further training. The 107th Tank Regiment, commanded by Col. Choe U Sik, along with the brigade's infantry, motorcycle, and training regiments remained at the original Sadong base. The 109th Tank Regiment, commanded by Col. Kim Tae Ryon was shipped to Chorwon, where the troops worked through December 1949 creating their own barracks. The 203rd Tank Regiment, led by the former commander of the 1st Battalion, 15th Tank Training Regiment, Col. Choe Ul Suk, was sent to Namchonjom.

The training in early 1950 consisted of instrument familiarization, operation of the tank radio and intercom system, operation of the 85mm gun and 7.62mm machine gun, and driving instruction. The crew members were taught only the skills needed for one position in the crew; there was no cross-training. Gunnery instruction was limited by parsimonious allotments of practice ammunition, and in general there was little or no practice in tank-vs.-tank fighting, since it was presumed that no enemy tanks would be encountered. Captured prisoners indicated that they had only fired two rounds of live main gun ammunition in pre-war practice. Although North Korean tanks did carry AP ammunition, the standard crew drill stressed the use of HE ammunition, which was the principal type used in the 105th Armored Brigade. Most of the units conducted three-day, battalion-level exercises prior to the start of the war. Further details of North Korean tank crew training are scant due to the severe losses suffered by the units in combat.

At the time of the North Korean invasion of South Korea in June 1950, the NKPA possessed 242 T-34-85 tanks, about half of them in the 105th Armored Brigade, including the 20 tanks with its 208th Tank Training Regiment. The remainder were intended as replacements or for new armor units. In contrast to the extensive training provided to the 105th Armored Brigade, the follow-on units received only hasty training (often as little as a month), mainly from the North Korean cadre. The 41st, 42nd, 43rd, 45th, and 46th Tank Regiments were actually understrength battalions seldom with more than 15 tanks each. Two more tank brigades were also being formed, the 16th and 17th, but they only reached tank regiment strength (about 40–45 tanks) by the time they were committed to action for the September 1 offensive on the Naktong River.

As well as the T-34-85 tanks, there were 176 SU-76M assault guns and 54 BA-64 armored cars. Besides their employment in the tank units, the SU-76M assault gun battalions were also attached to several of the frontline North Korean infantry divisions for fire support. They were sometimes called *Samouth* by the NKPA troops, a corruption of the Russian *samokhodnaya ustanovka* ("self-propelled carriage").

TRAINING THE US TANK FORCE

The US Army and Marine Corps underwent a substantial demobilization after the end of World War II. The army's size fell from eight million men in late 1945 to about one million in 1947, and of that figure nearly 400,000 belonged to the newly independent US Air Force. Major armored forces deployed overseas amounted to only three US Constabulary brigades in occupied Germany and four tank companies attached to the occupation divisions in Japan, equipped with the M24 Chaffee light tank. Worsening relations with the Soviet Union encouraged the US government to halt the military decline and to begin a gradual rebuilding of army strength. This program eventually included the conversion of the three Constabulary brigades in Germany into armored cavalry regiments, the creation of the 3rd Armored Cavalry Regiment in the United States, and the strengthening of the 2nd Armored Division. On paper, each infantry division was supposed to have an organic tank battalion, but as will be seen later, this had not necessarily taken place by 1950.

The US Army wrote off a large number of tanks immediately after the end of hostilities due to age or damage, and by the end of 1945 was down to about 29,000 tanks. Of these, 6,426 were disposed of by the end of June 1949, some via foreign aid contributions and further demilitarization. The table opposite shows the holdings at the end of June 1949, broken down into holdings in the US Zone of the Interior (ZI) and overseas. These total holdings were far in excess of the US Army's actual force structure

US Marine tank battalions were based on the M4A3 (105mm) howitzer tank until the Korean War. Although replaced in the tank platoons by the M26 Pershing for the Korea fighting, they still remained in use in the headquarters in a support role, fitted with a dozer blade, as seen here in the fighting near Yongsan on August 18, 1950. An M26 Pershing is in front. (NARA)

requirements, so in 1949 the Army Field Forces prepared a report for a "Balanced Tank Program," which planned to cut the inventory by more than half, some of the tanks being transferred as further foreign aid, and others converted as recovery vehicles.

US Army tank crew training remained centered on the Armored School at Ft. Knox. However, the miniscule size of the armored force in the postwar years led to a greatly shrunken program. During the Korean War, the US Army depended heavily on veteran tank crews still in uniform since World War II, or reservists called up after the outbreak of the war. So, for example, the commanders of the first four US Army tank battalions deployed to Korea were all experienced tank commanders. The 6th Tank Battalion was led by Lt. Col. John S. Growdon, who had served in the headquarters of the 9th Armored Division; the 70th Tank Battalion was commanded by Lt. Col. William Rodgers, who commanded a tank battalion in the Pacific theater in World War II; the 73rd Tank Battalion was led by Lt. Col. Calvin Hannum, who had served in the wartime headquarters of the 2nd Armored Division; the 89th Tank Battalion was commanded by Lt. Col. Welborn Dolvin, who commanded the 191st Tank Battalion in World War II. Indeed, the combat experience of the US tankers would be a major factor in the success of US tank units in action against the North Korean tank force in 1950. While most enlisted men in both the army and Marine Corps were recent inductees, tank units had a disproportionate share of NCOs, many of whom were WWII veterans. In the case of the army tank battalions, many of the NCOs had served in training units.

Although the individual skills of US tankers were considerably better than those of their North Korean counterparts, any organizational advantages were almost entirely lacking. The first units to see combat were separate tank companies of the four infantry divisions in Japan. These were equipped with M24 light tanks, which were incapable of dealing with the T-34-85 and were brushed aside while incurring heavy

US tank postwar inventory, 1945–50

	Dec 31, 1945 total	1949, ZI	1949, OS	1949 Total	1950 plan
M22, M5A1 light tank	4,337	964	0	964	0
M24 light tank	4,962	3,379	454	3,833	3,833
M4 (75mm) medium tank	6,933	5,455	156	5,611	0
M4 (76mm) medium tank	6,582	5,635	65	5,700	3,688
M4 (105mm) howitzer tank	3,731	2,886	97	2,983	0
M26 medium tank	1,918	1,523	378	1,901	0
M45 (105mm) howitzer tank	185	183	0	183	183
M46 medium tank	0	18	0	18	810
Other 90mm tank	0	49	0	49	47
Flamethrower, other tanks	n/a	151	0	151	149
Total	**28,648**	**20,243**	**1,150**	**21,393**	**8,710**

ZI = Zone of the Interior; OS = Overseas

casualties. In the wake of the disastrous pummeling of American and South Korean units in early July, the US Army began mobilizing tank units to rush to Korea. There were very few tank battalions near strength. The 6th Tank Battalion had been reactivated on January 31, 1949, and was equipped with the new M46 medium tank. Two more training battalions were also available: the 70th Tank Battalion, which was the training battalion at Ft. Knox with M4A3 and M26 tanks, and the 73rd Tank Battalion with M26 tanks from the infantry school at Ft. Benning. As well as these three battalions, the Eighth Army in Japan managed to scrape together 54 rebuilt M4A3E8 Shermans and form them into the 8072nd (later the 89th) Medium Tank Battalion. The first company from this unit arrived in Korea in late July and was committed to combat on August 2, 1950. The Marine Corps activated Co. A of the 1st Marine Brigade, and reequipped it with M26 Pershing tanksreplacing the previously-equipped M4A3(105) howitzer tanks. This company was attached to the 1st Marine Provisional Brigade. Later in the summer, the entire brigade was dispatched to Korea to serve under the re-activated Marine 1st Division. These tank units began to reach the embattled Pusan perimeter at the southeastern tip of the Korean peninsula in early to mid-August 1950.

The experiences of the 70th Tank Battalion illustrate the haste with which the units were mobilized. Lt. Col. Bill Rodgers received a phone call on Monday morning, July 8, 1950, and was told that he had been placed in command of the battalion and that it would depart for an unspecified foreign assignment that Friday, five days later. Tank Cos. A and C had 22 M4A3E8 Shermans each, and Co. B had 22 M26 Pershings, all old and beat-up tanks used for training. The companies were being used by the Armor School at Ft. Knox for gunnery, driving, communications, and recovery training, as well as for tank–infantry team demonstrations. To bolster tank strength, some M26 tanks that had been parked as monument tanks around the base were hastily sent through maintenance, and Rock Island Arsenal dispatched additional Shermans to the port of embarkation to make up for the worn-out tanks. All the tank companies were short-staffed, and tank crews were hastily dispatched from various units at Fort Campbell, Fort Meade and Fort Knox to bring the unit up to strength.

The battalion departed Ft. Knox, Kentucky, on July 17 by train cross-continent, arrived at Camp Stoneman, California, on July 20, departed Fort Mason by transport ship on July 23 and arrived in the Pusan perimeter on August 7. Lt. Col. Rodgers later remarked: "We sailed on a ship with two other tank battalions, the 6th and the 73rd, whose men had the same kind of hectic stories to tell. We landed at Pusan and went straight into combat, a complete bunch of strangers with no training." The battalion began to deploy towards Taegu on August 13, a little over a month after mobilization. One of the unit's enlisted men recalled that "Many of the men had stayed in the Army following World War II, and other like myself had joined the peacetime army but never thought we would be called on to go to war, certainly not in Korea. But here we were on this little train headed north from Pusan to Taegu where we would unload and soon be tested in the fire of combat."

The situation with the US Marine tanks was essentially the same. In July 1950, the USMC mobilized its 1st Marine Provisional Brigade to rush to Korea. The brigade's armor attachment, Co. A, 1st Tank Battalion, was the only active-duty Marine tank company on the west coast. It was commanded by Capt. Gearl M. English, a veteran World War II tanker, like his army counterparts. He had crewed an M2A4 light tank with one of the early Marine tank deployments (Co. A, 2nd Tank Battalion) in 1941 in Iceland and served through much of the war as an instructor at the Marine Tank School at Jacques' Farm. In 1944, he was assigned as a platoon leader with Co. C, 4th Tank Battalion and saw combat on Roi-Namur, Saipan, and Tinian, and earned the Silver Star during the violent fighting on Iwo Jima in 1945.

Co. A was normally equipped with M4A3 tanks, but for deployment to Korea it drew M26 Pershings from the Barstow Marine tank depot. The Marine Corps had obtained 102 Pershings from the army, but most Marine units, including Co. A, continued to use the M4A3 (105mm) howitzer tank for peacetime training. The only Pershing tanks in the battalion prior to Korea were in the HQ and Services Company, but it had been battalion practice in 1948–49 to rotate tank crews through this unit to acquaint them with the new tank. Conversion to the Pershing was not overly

difficult, as the fire controls and engine were the same as the M4A3. As in the case of the army tank battalions, the company was brought up to full strength on the eve of its deployment by calling in Marine tankers from posts scattered around the United States. The company had just one day on the tank ranges to become familiar with the new tank, and each gunner/loader team was able to fire only two rounds of 90mm ammunition. Although the company had a nominal strength of 22 tanks, five extra tanks had been dispatched for the tank platoon attached to the Marine regiment, at least on paper, and these were manned by the company headquarters staff.

The company arrived at Pusan on August 2, 1950, and was immediately dispatched to the front line. Time was so short that the company completed its first gunnery practice and gun bore-sighting from the railroad flatcars moving them to the front. As will be recounted later, this company was the first of the stateside replacements to encounter the T-34-85 in combat.

THE STRATEGIC SITUATION

Korea had been occupied by US and Soviet forces in 1945, with the Red Army north of the 38th Parallel, and the US Army to the south. With the onset of the Cold War, both areas set up their own rival governments, with promises to unify the country under each government's respective control. The US Army largely abandoned South Korea in 1949 except for small training detachments. Although the Republic of Korea (ROK) had begun to set up its own ROK Army (ROKA), the US government was

The ROK Army had no tanks and only light armored vehicles. This M3 half-track of the 1st Capitol Division is seen in action on July 7, 1950, during the opening phase of the conflict. It has a locally improvised .50-cal. heavy machine-gun pulpit on the right side. (NARA)

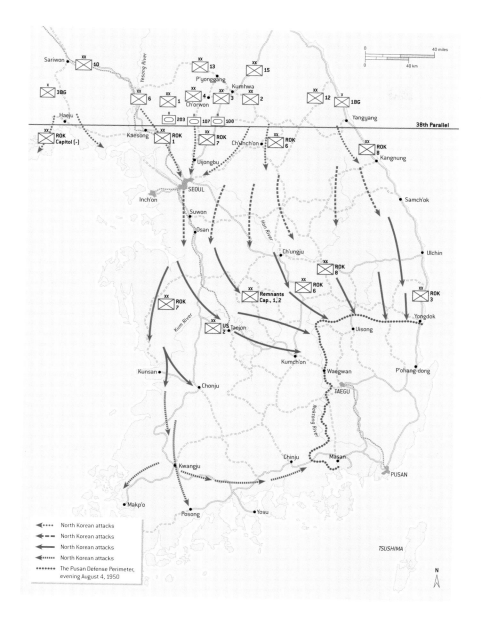

Legend:

North Korean attacks
North Korean attacks
North Korean attacks
North Korean attacks
The Pusan Defense Perimeter,
evening August 4, 1950

reluctant to provide it with offensive weapons more powerful than small arms because of concerns that the Syngman Rhee government would attempt to reunify the country by force. The Soviet Union and China in the meantime had equipped the NKPA with the full understanding that the Kim Il-Sung government had the same ambitions. Feckless US diplomacy led Stalin and Mao to conclude that Korea was outside the US sphere of influence after the 1949 troop withdrawals, and so gave the North Koreans the green light to initiate the war. War planning was conducted with Soviet assistance. Under the cover of peace negotiations, on June 12–23, the NKPA moved seven infantry divisions and the 105th Armored Brigade to within 10–15km (6–9 miles) of the 38th Parallel separating the two zones. The plan was based on a marked superiority

The principal anti-tank weapon of the ROK Army was the towed 57mm anti-tank gun, an American copy of the British 6-pdr. This gun had limited capability against the T-34-85, except against the side armor. This ROK Army 57mm gun is being towed by a ¾-ton truck during the evacuation of Suwon airbase in 1950. (NARA)

of the NKPA over the ROKA, with a 2:1 advantage in troops and rifles, a 7:1 advantage in machine guns, and a 13:1 advantage in submachine guns. The ROKA had no significant field artillery or tanks. The June plan, completed with Soviet assistance, expected that the NKPA would advance 15–20km (9–12 miles) per day and that the campaign would last 22–27 days.

While the NKPA tank force seems puny by today's standards, in 1950 this was the most formidable force in Asia except for that of the Soviet Army. Japan's armored force had been destroyed in the war, and China's force was a motley collection of

The standard US Army and Marine infantry support weapon in the Korean War was the M20 75mm recoilless rifle. This was often used in encounters with North Korean tanks, but was seldom effective, as its HE projectile had little armor-penetrating power. (NARA)

captured Japanese and American tanks. The US Army had no substantial tank force in occupied Japan beyond four companies of M24 Chaffee light tanks, and had withdrawn the medium tanks used in the occupation of South Korea in 1949. South Korea had no tank force and its only armored vehicles were 37 M8 armored cars and a small number of M3 half-tracks of a cavalry regiment of the 1st Capitol Division in Seoul. Anti-tank weapons were poor and consisted of 140 ineffective 57mm anti-tank guns – an American copy of the British 6-pdr – and about 1,900 2.36in bazookas.

The NKPA planned to use the 105th Armored Brigade as the spearhead of its invasion of South Korea. Korea is an extremely mountainous country, particularly along its eastern coast. The traditional invasion route has been along the western coast, as the mountains gradually give way to a coastal plain. Equally importantly, the South Korean capital of Seoul was located in this area, so it was the natural destination of the 105th Armored Brigade. Contrary to Soviet doctrine, the brigade did not fight as a single unit, but its regiments were doled out to support NKPA infantry divisions.

COMBAT

The lead NKPA tank unit was the 109th Tank Regiment, commanded by Col. Kim Tae Ryon, which was attached to the NKPA 3rd Infantry Division. These formations were the first across the border at 0500hrs on June 25, 1950, near Sachang-Ni in the westernmost section of South Korea. This unit overran the ROK 17th Infantry Regiment, and other NKPA units soon followed. Col. Choe Ul Suk's 203rd Tank Regiment was attached to the NKPA's 1st Infantry Division, and attacked along the Kaesong–Seoul "Unification" highway. The 107th Tank Regiment led by Col. Choe

The T-34-85 terrorized the poorly equipped ROK infantry units and proved itself the dominant weapon in the opening phase of the Korean War. This is a T-34-85 of the commander of the 4th Company, 2nd Tank Battalion, 203rd Tank Regiment, 105th Tank Brigade, shortly after the capture of Seoul in July 1950.

U Sik overran the ROK 12th Regiment of the 1st Infantry Division at Kaesong and the 13th Regiment near a ford over the Imjin River near Korangpo. South Korean troops claim to have knocked out 11 T-34 tanks during the Imjin fighting, but later interrogations of NKPA tankers revealed that none had been lost, although several had been damaged. The 107th Tank Regiment, supporting the NKPA 4th Infantry Division, attacked along the Yonchon–Seoul road, to the east of the other two tank regiments. It crushed several units of the ROK 7th Infantry Division.

Most South Korean troops had never seen a tank before, and the ineffectiveness of their 57mm guns and 2.36in bazookas was demoralizing. Several Korean infantry units attempted to stop the tanks with improvised satchel charges or TNT blocks wrapped around grenades, at high cost – some 90 soldiers of the 1st Division alone were killed using these desperate tactics. The helplessness of the South Korean infantry at the hands of the North Korean tanks led to "tank panic," which eroded the ROK's resistance.

After overcoming the remaining defenses of the ROK 7th Infantry Division, the NKPA 107th and 109th Tank Regiments met up on June 27 at Uijongbu, which served as the staging point for the main attack on Seoul. Following the capture of Seoul on June 28, the brigade moved to the Han River. In panic, the ROK Army prematurely blew the main railroad bridge over the river, with heavy ROK traffic still on it, killing several hundred soldiers and civilian refugees. This catastrophe left significant elements of the ROK Army trapped on the northern side of the Han River, along with most of their heavy equipment, and they were quickly overcome. The NKPA engineers now needed several days to improvise means for the tanks to cross the river. The first tanks were not across until July 3, and the 109th Tank Regiment took part in the capture of the port of Inchon the same day.

In the meantime, the US Army began mobilizing forces to rush to Korea, and won United Nations (UN) approval for a multinational campaign. The first source of troops was units stationed on occupation duty in Japan. Task Force Smith from the 24th Infantry Division was the first to arrive, consisting of about 400 infantrymen. On July 5, the NKPA had its first encounter with Task Force Smith near Osan, when the US infantry unit was attacked by 33 T-34-85 tanks of the 107th Tank Regiment. US 105mm howitzers began engaging the tanks with HE ammunition, which killed many NKPA infantry riding the tanks Soviet-style but failed to stop the tanks themselves. A 105mm howitzer battery, however, waited until the tanks were within 500 yards (457m) and managed to knock out the two lead T-34-85 tanks using high-explosive anti-tank (HEAT) ammunition. Yet there were only six HEAT rounds available, which were quickly exhausted. US troops also fired on the tanks with two 75mm recoilless rifles, which proved useless. The battalion's main anti-tank weapon, the 2.36in bazooka, was equally ineffective, and no fewer than 22 rockets were fired without effect. The Task Force managed to disable only four tanks before being forced to retreat. Task Force Smith lost about 150 men, over a third of its strength, in the one-sided battle.

The 34th Infantry was the first large US unit to arrive at the battlefront, and deployed around Chonan. When attacked by T-34-85 tanks on July 8, the regimental commander, Col. Bob Martin, attempted to rally his dispirited troops in the street fighting. After grabbing a bazooka, he faced down a T-34-85 tank in the town, but the rocket failed to stop the tank. He was blown in half by tank fire at close range; the US positions disintegrated against the relentless tank assaults.

On July 9, the NKPA's 105th Armored Brigade, recently given the honorific title of 105th Seoul Tank Division, was united near Suwon for further operations. Up to this time, the brigade had only lost two tanks to mines and two more in the fighting with Task Force Smith. The NKPA's heaviest armor losses occurred on June 28, when seven of the brigade's 16 SU-76M assault guns were knocked out by counter-battery fire from the 105mm howitzers of the ROK 6th Infantry Division near Chunchon. By now, the UN operation to thwart the NKPA invasion was beginning to take shape, but American air actions against the armored spearheads in early July were ineffective, contrary to pilots' claims.

The four US Army divisions with the Eighth Army in Japan – the 7th, 24th, 25th Infantry, and 1st Cavalry – nominally each had an attached tank battalion, respectively the 77th, 78th, 79th, and 71st Tank Battalions. But because of the narrow roads and delicate bridges in Japan, they in fact only had a single company from each battalion, equipped with the M24 Chaffee light tank. These were rushed to Korea.

On July 20, 1950, during the hasty defense of Taejon, the commander of the US 24th Infantry Division led a detachment to prove that the newly arrived 3.5in bazooka could stop a T-34-85. This is one of two tanks knocked out by Dean's group that day, the first small victory against NKPA armor. (NARA)

The first of these units to see combat was Co. A, 78th Heavy Tank Battalion, which supported the 21st Infantry Regiment of the 24th Infantry Division at Chonjui on July 10. The M24s were hopelessly outclassed by the Korean T-34-85s; they scored several direct hits on the enemy tanks, but only disabled one. Two M24s were lost in the first day of fighting when their poorly maintained gun recoil systems malfunctioned, wrecking the guns and the turrets. Three more M24s were lost the following day. The M24 was vulnerable not only to the T-34's 85mm gun, but also the NKPA's 14.5mm PTRS anti-tank rifles, which the American tankers labeled "buffalo guns." The poor performance of the M24 against the T-34-85s demoralized the crews, and the tankers proved to be very skittish in supporting the infantry in the ensuing battles for the Kum River line, even without NKPA tank opposition. By August, only two tanks of the original 14 in the company were left. The other two tank companies were also roughly handled: Co. A, 71st Tank Battalion, lost most of its tanks by early August, and Co. A, 79th Tank Battalion, suffered in several unequal skirmishes with T-34-85s. US Army commanders soon lost confidence in tank support and pleaded instead for better anti-tank weapons. Supplies of 3.5in "super-bazookas" were airlifted to Korea in mid-July.

The first Pershing tanks to see combat in Korea were found in Tokyo depots and hastily shipped to Korea. They were used to form a provisional tank company, but during their first engagement at Chinju against the NKPA 6th Infantry Division on July 28, all were lost due to mechanical breakdowns. This photo of the unit was taken during training at Taegu on July 20, 1950. There is an M24 Chaffee and an M8 armored car in the background.

NKPA infantry from the 3rd and 4th Divisions overcame US resistance along the Kum River without tank support in mid-July. The 107th Tank Regiment moved across the river around July 16 to support the assault on the surviving elements of the US Army 24th Infantry Division at Taejon. The battle of Taejon was the first time that 3.5in bazookas were available, and they were first used in action on July 20, knocking out two T-34-85 tanks in the first encounter. Through the course of the day, tank-hunting teams destroyed or disabled several more T-34-85s in the streets of Taejon. They included a team led by the divisional commander, Maj. Gen. William F. Dean. Dean took the personal lead in an urban tank-hunting mission to convince his troops that the new bazookas could destroy the previously invincible T-34 tanks, especially in the close confines of a town. The NKPA lost about 15 tanks in the fighting for Taejon, its heaviest armored losses to date. Seven of these were due to bazookas and five were caused by air attacks. Nevertheless, the 24th Infantry Division suffered about 30 percent casualties in the fighting, including Gen. Dean, and Taejon was lost.

THE PUSAN PERIMETER

With the fall of Taejon on July 20, US and South Korean forces pulled back over the Naktong River to the Pusan perimeter at the southeasternmost tip of Korea, there to await further UN reinforcements. The main cause of North Korean tank casualties in late July was the poor road conditions in the mountainous country leading towards the Pusan perimeter. The tanks began to show the first signs of wear caused by the

The first US medium tank unit to see extensive combat was the 8072nd Tank Battalion, later renamed the 89th Tank Battalion. This M4A3E8 of Co. B supported the 25th Infantry Division in the Pusan perimeter on August 9, 1950. (NARA)

intensive actions of the previous weeks of fighting and by the harsh terrain; some tanks had to be cannibalized for parts. More heavy losses were suffered at Kumchon on July 23, when several tanks were destroyed in minefields and several more knocked out by bazookas during a bloody battle with the "Wolfhounds" of the 27th Infantry. This was the first time an NKPA armored attack had been stopped by US infantry and proved the effectiveness of the new 3.5in bazookas in the hands of determined troops. The minefields and infantry resistance delayed the NKPA tank advance, and on July 28 the UN airstrikes finally began to take effect, when at least five tanks were knocked out by rocket and napalm attacks. By early August, the operational strength of the North Korean armored brigade was down to only about 40 T-34-85 tanks, with many others waiting by the roadside for repair. Although the air attacks did not destroy the number of tanks claimed, they did disrupt the supply of spare parts and replacement tanks.

The air attacks led the North Korean armored brigade to change its tactics, and large-scale movements were confined to night to avoid the UN aircraft. Attempts to cross the Naktong River were rebuffed at least twice by US aircraft, which claimed another five tanks. In the meantime, another US tank action took place. Three broken-down M26 Pershing tanks had been discovered at the Tokyo Ordnance Depot and were quickly refurbished and shipped to Korea. They formed a provisional tank platoon alongside a small number of M24 Chaffees, and were used in attempts to defend Chinju from the NKPA 6th Infantry Division on July 28. However, they broke down during the fighting and were abandoned.

The Marine Corps' Co. A, 1st Tank Battalion, was the first of the stateside units to arrive in Pusan, on August 2, 1950, and the first to be sent into combat. The four US Army tank battalions mobilized in July 1950 also began to reach the embattled Pusan perimeter by mid-August. The first army medium tank unit in action was the 89th Tank Battalion, equipped with three companies of M4A3E8s and one of M26 Pershings; the surviving M24s of the 79th Tank Battalion were attached as a fifth company. The battalion's introduction to combat was not auspicious. A tank company

The 72nd Tank Battalion was the first unit to arrive in Korea with any significant number of M26 tanks; this one named "Margaret" of Co. C is in action on the Pusan perimeter on August 27, 1950.

of M4A3E8 Shermans led an attack near Masan on August 2, and were ambushed by an NKPA 45mm anti-tank platoon, which knocked out eight tanks in quick succession. The battalion saw no further tank fighting in early August, but was extensively and successfully used in support of local infantry actions.

As US Army and Marine tank strength began building up in the Pusan perimeter, the UN forces began to conduct a more vigorous defense, including some local counterattacks. The tide was beginning to turn very slowly in favor of the UN and the US Army was regaining its confidence in its tank units.

The NKPA 105th Armored Brigade finally made it across the Naktong River and took part in the attacks on Taegu on August 12, 1950. The 2nd Battalion of the 109th Tank Regiment was decimated by severe UN air attacks on Chonjui around August 13, with the regiment losing 20 tanks and having several more damaged. The surviving tanks of the 105th Armored Brigade were dispersed, and they supported NKPA infantry assaults on towns all along the Pusan perimeter rather than being concentrated for one major blow. Finally, on August 15, an independent tank battalion with 21 T-34-85 tanks from the Sadong tank training center arrived to make up for the losses of the previous weeks of fighting. During the crossing of the Naktong river near Waegwan, the brigade was again subjected to merciless air attack.

DUEL AT OBONG-NI RIDGE

US Marine tanks were the first to defeat the invincible NKPA T-34-85s. By mid-August 1950, the North Korean offensive was running out of steam in the face of increasing resistance from US and ROK forces. The first US/ROK efforts to break out of the Pusan perimeter had begun on August 17, 1950, with attacks towards the Naktong River. The 5th Regiment of the 1st Provisional Marine Brigade was assigned to seize the Obong-Ni Ridge, better known to the Marines as "No Name Ridge,"

This photo of a pair of M26s of Co. A, Marine 1st Tank Battalion, was probably taken on August 18, 1950, a day after the duel near Obong-Ni Ridge (the ridge can be seen in the background). The T-34-85 at left is number 314, the tank of the commander of the NKPA 2nd Tank Battalion, 109th Tank Regiment. It escaped the initial ambush, but was hit by bazooka fire from the US Army 9th Infantry soldiers holding the hill to the north. It suffered a turret ammunition fire that blew off the roof, as can clearly be seen. (NARA)

a mile-long series of hills averaging about 107m (350ft) in elevation. On the northern flank was the US Army's 9th Infantry Regiment. The infantry were supported by a platoon of four M26 Pershing tanks of Co. A, Marine 1st Tank Battalion, led by Lt. Granville Sweet. Opposing them was the NKPA 4th Infantry Division, supported by the 2nd Battalion, 109th Tank Regiment.

The fighting that day was dominated by infantry actions, with the American assault supported both by artillery and airstrikes. By early evening, the 5th Marines and the US 9th Infantry began to set up defensive positions for the night. Around 2000hrs, Lt. Sweet received the radio message "Flash Purple," the Marine code for imminent tank attack. The Pershing tanks were in the process of refueling, and they moved forward individually as they completed this task. Up to this time, the T-34-85 tanks had proven invincible, but Sweet was determined that his platoon would halt the North Korean drive, if only by blocking the road through a narrow defile with the hulks of their tanks. The 1/5th Marines had set up a tank ambush, though there was

DUEL AT OBONG-NI RIDGE (OVERLEAF)

Lt. Granville Sweet's platoon of four M26 Pershing tanks of Co. A, Marine 1st Tank Battalion, was refueling when a radio alarm was received: "Flash Purple" — the Marine code for an enemy tank attack. Sweet rushed his tanks forward and deployed them in a narrow defile in the road, so that even if his tanks were knocked out they would block the road and prevent the onrushing T-34-85 tanks from passing behind Marine lines. The T-34-85 had dominated the Korean battlefield since the start of the invasion a month earlier, and had never been soundly defeated in battle. The Marines had no idea whether their 90mm guns could penetrate the armor of the opposing tanks.

The platoon of four T-34-85 tanks of 2nd Battalion, 109th Tank Regiment, advanced down a road between the positions of the US Army 9th Infantry Regiment to the north, and the 5th Marines to the south, and threatened to cut behind American lines. Bazooka and recoilless rifle teams fired on the tanks, setting their external fuel tanks on fire but failing to stop them.

When the first T-34-85 turned around the corner of the hill, it was confronted by a solid steel phalanx of M26 tanks blocking the road. Three of the Pershings were arranged in a line from left to right, consisting of TSgt. Cecil Fullerton's A-34, Sgt. Gerald Swinicke's A-33, and Sgt. Basilo Chavarria's A-32, with Sweet's tank (A-31) behind them. Sweet's tank had a problem with the gun elevation mechanism, and so would take no direct part in the duel.

Fullerton's tank spotted the first North Korean tank to round the bend and began engaging it with HVAP ammunition. After the first three rounds were fired, Fullerton complained to his gunner, Sgt. Stanley Tarnowski, "You missed, Ski!" Tarnowski replied "I don't miss, Sergeant Fullerton." Tarnowski had a reputation in the unit as a crack shot, and it would be hard to miss at point-blank range. In fact, the HVAP was such an overmatch for the T-34-85 glacis armor at such short range that the rounds had passed through the tank.

The first round had struck the glacis near the hull machine gun, killing the gunner and killing or wounding the loader before punching through the rear plate. Marines on a neighboring hill thought they themselves were under fire when the three rounds impacted near them. Curiously enough, the Marine tanks then burst into flames, though not from enemy action. In the haste to finish refueling, a considerable amount of gas had been spilled on the decks of some of the Pershings. The initial gun blasts ignited the gasoline fumes; these were extinguished by the subsequent gun blast, only to be ignited by the next shot in a curious pyrotechnic display.

The second T-34-85 foolishly continued past the stalled lead tank and was hit by a volley of fire from the Marine tanks. One round struck the turret, which swung uncontrollably to the left, firing its gun into the banking. The third T-34-85 attempted to fire back past the wrecks of the two other tanks, but was soon pummeled by seven rounds of APC and HVAP. Three of the crew escaped from the stricken tank, but were killed by small-arms fire. The Marines kept pouring fire into the tanks to set them ablaze, until ordered to stop by Lt. Sweet. The skirmish had lasted less than ten minutes. Accounts of the action vary, with some reports claiming that the NKPA tanks repeatedly fired back at the Pershings, but the brigade after-action report states that the NKPA tanks fired only two rounds. The fourth NKPA tank, that of the 2nd Battalion commander in tank 314, escaped down the road, but was knocked out by an army bazooka team from the neighboring F Co., 9th Infantry.

The Marines later surmised that the North Koreans had continued to advance because they thought they were only facing the puny M24 tanks encountered over the previous weeks. The lead T-34-85 tanks did not burn when first hit, so the following tanks did not realize the danger they faced. Assuming, therefore, that they were impervious to the 75mm guns of the M24, they continued to advance, only to be blasted by the 90mm guns.

These are two of the three T-34-85 tanks of the 109th Tank Regiment knocked out in the fighting near the Obong-Ni Ridge, but pushed off the road after the skirmish. The tank to the left has suffered an ammunition fire in the turret, which has blown off the roof. (NARA)

little confidence that it would do much good against the North Korean tanks. A company of 75mm recoilless rifles was positioned on a small elevation dubbed "Observation Hill," with a clear field of fire towards the road. Marine positions forward of the tank platoon had deployed their 3.5in bazooka teams on Hill 125, which covered the road on the north side.

The North Korean column was first hit by an air attack by Marine F4U Corsairs, which stripped away some of the accompanying infantry; the Marine pilots also claimed to have damaged one T-34-85 tank. The Marines on Hill 125 now began firing bazooka rockets at the lead tanks of the NKPA column, the rockets setting some of the tanks' external fuel tanks on fire. The T-34-85s, however, continued to advance, in spite of the damage. Sweet radioed his platoon to try using the new HVAP against the approaching armor. As the tanks rounded the corner, they were pummeled by a volley of tank fire at point-blank range. The Marines knocked out the three lead T-34-85 tanks; the battalion commander in the last tank tried to escape back down the road, but his tank was stopped by army bazookas.

Technical Sergeant Cecil Fullerton's tank, number A-34, advances into Yongsan on September 3, 1950, during the efforts to repulse the NKPA September 1 offensive against the Naktong bulge. Fullerton's tank had been the first to fire on the advancing T-34-85 tanks during the Obong-Ni Ridge duel two weeks before. (NARA)

The official Marine history later recalled that the duel had "shattered the myth of the T-34 in five flaming minutes." The T-34-85, once dreaded as invincible, was now derisively called the "Caviar Can." The NKPA attack had employed careless tactics. Until this point in the war, the T-34-85 had had nothing to fear from any weapon, so the Korean tankers were overconfident. The Marine tankers were surprised that the T-34-85s continued to advance around the corner, even after the first tank had been hit. Nor were the Marines impressed with North Korean gunnery skills. The NKPA tank crews seemed unprepared for action and failed to respond quickly enough once the firefight began.

The duel near the Obong-Ni Ridge also reinforces a conclusion of operational research on tank-vs.-tank fighting in World War II: the tank that sees the enemy first and fires first is the most likely winner of the duel. A study of US tank engagements in Korea concluded that the M26 had an effectiveness rating of 33.1 when firing first, but only 0.5 when firing second in tank duels (combat effectiveness was assessed as the ratio of tank losses vs. tank kills along with the relative number of enemy and friendly tanks). Not surprisingly, tanks in a defensive position consistently had a significant advantage in tank duels since they tended to locate and engage first against an approaching opponent. Overall, tanks firing from defensive positions tended to be three times more effective in the US case, and two times more effective in the case of the North Koreans.

The NKPA partly redeemed its fumbling attack a few weeks later on September 5, 1950, when two more T-34-85s supported by a pair of SU-76M assault guns and a company of infantry attacked the same location. The M26 tanks of the 1st Platoon rushed forward, but with their turrets facing in the wrong direction; both were hit by 85mm fire and knocked out. The NKPA armored vehicles, however, were also all knocked out with bazooka fire.

M26 Pershings of the 1st Marine Tank Battalion in action on September 3, 1950. An observer is on the ground between the two tanks, but he would evacuate his position before they fired to avoid concussion from the muzzle blast. That day, the Marine tanks took part in fighting against the new NKPA 16th Armored Brigade, knocking out several T-34-85s near Yongsan.

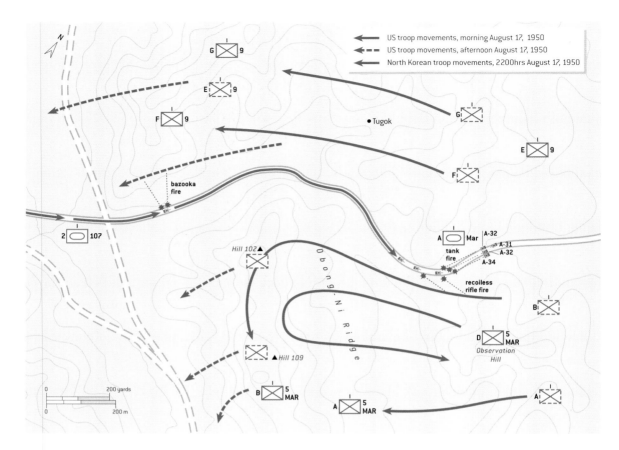

US troop movements, morning August 17, 1950
US troop movements, afternoon August 17, 1950
North Korean troop movements, 2200hrs August 17, 1950

G | 9
E | 9
F | 9
G | 9
E | 9
F | 9

• Tugok

bazooka fire

2 | 107

Hill 102 ▲

Obong-Ni Ridge

▲ Hill 109

A | Mar
A-32
A-31
tank fire
A-32
A-34
recoiless rifle fire

B |

D | 5 MAR
Observation Hill

B | 5 MAR

A | 5 MAR

A |

0   200 yards
0   200 m

The duel at Obong-Ni Ridge. August 17, 1950

THE "BOWLING ALLEY"

The next heavy tank action took place further north near Tabu-dong, where the US Army 27th Infantry Regiment was attacking to relieve pressure on Taegu. Co. C, 73rd Tank Battalion, was assigned to support the infantry. On the night of August 27, 1950, the NKPA began its last major tank action down a valley, with elements of the 107th Tank Regiment reinforced by some new tanks and crews from the Sadong tank

On the night of August 27, 1950, the NKPA 107th Tank Regiment began its last major tank action down the "Bowling Alley" near Taegu against the US Army 27th Infantry. It was stopped by tank fire from Pershings of Co. C, 73rd Tank Battalion. Here, after the fighting, an M26 Pershing drives past some of the North Korean wrecks. (NARA)

Two T-34-85 tanks of the NKPA 16th Armored Brigade, knocked out by Marine M26 Pershings during fighting near Yongsan on September 3–4, are inspected by men of Co. B, 1/5th Marines. The nearest tank has taken a hit on the front side of the turret, which evidently led to a vehicle fire that burned out the tank. This particular tank is an example of the 1945–46 production at Omsk Plant No. 174. (NARA)

school. Tracer fire came barreling down the road through the center of the valley, leading to its nickname the "Bowling Alley." The NKPA attack was stopped by the infantry and Pershing tanks, and in two days of fighting the North Koreans lost 13 T-34-85 tanks and five SU-76M assault guns.

After the tank skirmishes, it became increasingly risky for the NKPA to mass its armor, as the UN air forces had become much more prevalent over the Pusan perimeter and tanks were a high-priority target. The end of August saw the final commitment of the NKPA tank force. An assortment of partially formed tank regiments and brigades were sent south for an offensive intended to smash the Pusan

Troops of the 5th Cavalry inspect a knocked-out T-34-85 near Waegwan in September 1950. This tank is numbered 801, indicating that it is the tank of the commander of 1st Battalion, 16th Armored Brigade. (NARA)

Another T-34-85 of the 16th Armored Brigade knocked out in fighting in late September 1950 near Waegwan. It has suffered a turret ammunition fire, which has blown off its roof. (NARA)

perimeter, starting on September 1, 1950. In total, about 150 T-34-85 tanks had been committed to the initial assault on South Korea, and this second wave totaled about 100 tanks, but the crews were far more poorly trained than those of the elite 105th Armored Brigade.

The North Korean infantry, almost as poorly equipped as the ROKA as far as anti-tank weapons were concerned, would often try to overwhelm American tanks by massed infantry attacks, hoping to pry open a hatch. It was a costly tactic, but sometimes worked, especially at night or in close terrain. While the bulk of the NKPA attention was focused on the Pusan perimeter and the September Naktong offensive, a far more serious threat was about to strike the NKPA from behind.

THE INCHON LANDINGS

By September 1950, the UN forces in the Pusan perimeter had gained numerical superiority over the NKPA forces besieging them. The area outside the perimeter was very mountainous, however, and the UN commander, Gen. Douglas MacArthur, opted for a bolder approach to turn the tide against the North Koreans. In a brilliant gamble, X Corps was assigned to stage an amphibious landing behind the main NKPA forces at the port city of Inchon on the Yellow Sea coast west of Seoul. MacArthur hoped that the sudden appearance of a strong UN force at Seoul, deep in the NKPA rear, would cause the enemy to go into headlong retreat.

The X Corps assault formation for the Inchon landings was the 1st Marine Division, supported by the 1st Marine Tank Battalion, followed by the US Army 7th Infantry Division with its 73rd Tank Battalion. The landings began on September 16 using LVT-3 amtracs, since the coastal mud in the beach area was too thick for the Marines to wade ashore from landing craft. The assault forces landed in three areas: in the early morning at Green Beach on the Wolmi-do peninsula and in the afternoon at Red Beach and Blue Beach on either side of Wolmi-do. The ferocious tides in the

An M26 Pershing of the 72nd Tank Battalion, crowded with troops of the 9th Infantry, 2nd Infantry Division, moves forward during the fighting at Yongsan on September 3, 1950. These units were involved in the heavy fighting around Yongsan from September 1, the start of the NKPA's final Naktong offensive.

approaches to Inchon and the limited resources did not permit a simultaneous landing. Yet the only North Korean armor encountered in the initial landing at Wolmi-do was a BA-64 armored car, which was blown apart by a 90mm round from a Marine M26 Pershing.

The North Koreans had been warned of the planned landing by Soviet intelligence, based on information from British spies. Kim Il-Sung, however, ignored the warnings and concentrated instead on renewed attacks on the Pusan perimeter. The North Korean leader believed a collapse of the Pusan perimeter was imminent, and that the amphibious assault on Inchon and Seoul would be preempted by the need to rescue surviving US forces at Pusan. Instead, the US forces in Pusan were on the verge of breaking out, and Seoul was only weakly defended.

The NKPA only had the inexperienced 42nd Mechanized Regiment, with 18 T-34-85s, in the Seoul area. Yet once news arrived of MacArthur's assault, the 105th

A T-34-85 of the 42nd Mechanized Regiment, knocked out in fighting with Co. B, Marine 1st Tank Battalion, on September 16, 1950, near Red Beach outside Inchon. This NKPA unit had been sent from Sinuiju to Seoul in early September and had 18 T-34-85 tanks. It has the characteristic Gorkiy Plant No. 112 enlarged turret. (NARA)

An M26 Pershing of 1st Platoon, Co. B, Marine 1st Tank Battalion, leads an attack by a squad from 5th Marines on September 19 during the push from Kimpo airbase to the Han River.

Armored Brigade was ordered to withdraw back north, and the new 43rd Tank Regiment with 10–15 T-34-85s was transferred from Wonson. A company of fewer than ten T-34-85 tanks of the 42nd Mechanized Regiment tried to intervene during the late afternoon of September 16, but three were knocked out by airstrikes, and three more by Marine M26s. On September 17, 1950, six T-34-85 tanks, their crews still munching on their breakfasts, stumbled into the 5th Marines who were moving on Kimpo airbase. The Marines were supported by M26 Pershings of the 1st Marine Tank Battalion, and all six T-34-85s were destroyed in a storm of recoilless rifle and tank fire without loss to the Marines. A short time later, the burning NKPA column was passed by Gen. MacArthur, who commented "Considering that they're Russian, these tanks are in the condition I want them to be!"

M26 Pershings of Co. A, Marine 1st Tank Battalion, move into Seoul on September 26 to provide fire support for the Marine assault in the city. Much of the fighting in the center of Seoul, including the "battle of the barricades," was supported by M26 tanks of Co. B.

Most of the NKPA tanks in Inchon and Seoul were destroyed by Marine bazooka teams. A total of 24 T-34-85s were destroyed between September 16 and 20, eliminating the 42rd Mechanized Regiment. Another 12 T-34-85s from the 43rd Tank Regiment were knocked out on September 25, at least seven by Marine tanks. The main task of the Pershings in the Seoul fighting was providing close fire support during the street combat. The NKPA had erected barricades across most of the major streets, and the Marine tanks were used to help break up these defenses in savage street actions.

On September 20, Co. B, 73rd Tank Battalion, was supporting a drive by the 31st Infantry, but ran the gauntlet of North Korean defenses along the Suwon road, losing one M4A3E8 to Korean tank fire, but destroying eight T-34-85s. A portion of the unit later repulsed a North Korean tank attack near the airstrip, destroying three more T-34-85 tanks after they ran over four scout jeeps. In the final tank action by the battalion near Seoul, Co. A entered Suwon from the western side of the town, and knocked out four more T-34 tanks. The column, in support of Task Force Hannum, continued south towards Osan, where four more T-34-85s were encountered and destroyed.

BREAKOUT FROM THE PUSAN POCKET

While MacArthur was landing at Inchon, plans were underway for the Eighth Army to begin a breakout from the Pusan perimeter. The North Koreans had been reinforced opposite the pocket, prior to the beginning of the September 1 Naktong offensive, by the newly raised 16th and 17th Armored Regiments. The offensive, although very costly to both sides, had failed, and the NKPA was near breaking point. Its units were decimated and its troops exhausted and on the brink of starvation.

The Eighth Army counteroffensive was scheduled for a day after the Inchon landings (September 17), hoping to take advantage of panic amongst the North Korean troops after word of the Inchon landings reached them. The broad offensive was indeed aided by news of the Inchon landings arriving at NKPA headquarters, and, as expected, a general retreat northwards commenced. The North Korean units were ordered to fall back on Seoul, but many soldiers instead headed into the mountainous country along the eastern coast, realizing that the US forces were less likely to follow them there. By this time the 105th Armored Brigade was already withdrawing, based on previous orders. There were large numbers of T-34-85 tanks that had broken down during earlier offensives. Many of these vehicles had functional weapons, so

This T-34-85 of the 203rd Tank Regiment, 105th Armored Brigade, ran over several 7th Cavalry vehicles from Task Force Lynch before being hit by 3.5in bazooka fire tank fire from Co. C, 70th Tank Battalion, during the confused fighting near Suwon on September 27, 1950. (NARA)

One of the most unusual tank duels of the war took place on October 12, 1950, near Songhyon-Ni, when this T-34-85 suddenly appeared out of the fog and rammed an M4A3E8 tank of Co. B, 70th Tank Battalion. The Sherman backed up and fired a single shot, which split the Korean tank's gun barrel. A second US tank pulled alongside and destroyed the T-34-85 with a point-blank shot into the turret.

they were moved into defensive positions along key routes in the hopes of acting as improvised pillboxes to stop the UN advance.

The commander of the Eighth Army, Gen. Walton Walker, had served with George Patton in World War II, and he decided to use a mobile force to spearhead the link-up between the Pusan perimeter formations and MacArthur's X Corps in Seoul. He chose a battalion from the 7th Cavalry Regiment reinforced with seven M4A3E8 tanks from Co. C, 70th Tank Battalion. The spearhead was called Task Force Lynch.

The task force set out late on the night of September 21, with the objective of seizing the Naktong-Ni ferry crossing site 56km (35 miles) north of Tabu-dong. The motorized unit moved very quickly against light resistance. With tanks in the lead, the column was finally halted at Naksong-dong, when the two lead M4A3E8 tanks were knocked out by an emplaced 76mm gun. The gun position was overcome by infantry, however, and shortly afterwards Task Force Lynch encountered the rear elements of the retreating NKPA. An enemy ammunition train soon fell victim to tank fire, and a further 20 artillery piece, 50 ex-US Army trucks, and four T-34 tanks were captured. An NKPA infantry column was caught in the middle of the Naktong River and decimated.

The success of the Task Force in taking its objective led Gen. Walker to order it to continue its lightning advance to the northwest. In the lead was the 3rd Platoon, Co. C, 70th Tank Battalion, under Lt. Robert Baker. Baker's column linked up with X Corps' 73rd Tank Battalion near Suwon around midnight, September 26/27 – the first contact between the Pusan perimeter troops and MacArthur's Inchon force. Task Force Lynch had covered 164km (102 miles) in only 11 hours. Baker's tank platoon, however, had lost contact with the other elements of Task Force Lynch, which were still behind him. Later that night the task force was attacked by about ten T-34-85 tanks. The remaining tanks from 2nd Platoon, Co. C, 70th Tank Battalion, moved forwards from the rear of the task force to engage them. Two Shermans were quickly knocked out by two dug-in T-34-85s, but the third M4A3E8 moved forward and destroyed these. Another T-34-85 slipped into the infantry truck column and crushed about 15 jeeps and trucks, before finally being destroyed by a 105mm howitzer at a range of 10 yards (11m). Four other T-34s were destroyed by bazooka teams. That afternoon, two surviving T-34-85s were chased through the villages of Habung-Ni and Pyongtaek, where they were finally hit from the rear by tank fire from the 70th Tank Battalion. This encounter was the largest tank-vs.-tank engagement during the break-out.

On October 27, 1950, another amphibious landing was undertaken at Wonson, on the eastern coast of Korea, by the 1st Marine Division. By this time, the NKPA was in total disarray, and the landing was unopposed. The M26 tanks of Co. D, Marine 1st Tank Battalion, were fitted with the full deep-wading trunks for the operation, to allow the tanks to be landed in the shallow harbor from Landing Ship, Utility (LSU) vessels. Here, one of the tanks sits near the airbase with its wading trunks still attached. (NARA)

The best-equipped US Army tank unit, the 6th Tank Battalion, had the new M46 tanks, but saw very little tank fighting until October 22, when Co. A encountered eight T-34-85s and one SU-76M and knocked them all out in a brief and one-sided firefight. Eight other T-34-85s were found shortly afterward, all abandoned by their crews.

FINAL TANK BATTLES

The heaviest tank-vs.-tank fighting of the Korean War took place from August to October 1950. There were hardly any encounters with North Korean armor after November 1950, although the US Army and Marine Corps continued to make extensive use of tanks for infantry support for the remaining two years of the conflict. Other UN forces also employed tanks during the fighting, including British Centurion, Churchill, and Cromwell tanks, and Canadian Shermans. The only British tank duel of the war was fought between a Centurion and a Cromwell tank that had been captured by the Chinese.

M46 tanks of the newly arrived 64th Tank Battalion take up defensive positions at Kagae-dong in support of the 3rd Infantry Division, in an attempt to stem the tide of the Chinese advance on December 7, 1950. The 3rd Infantry Division had moved into the Hamhung–Wonsan area in November to relieve the 1st Marine Division, which was moving forward towards the Chosin reservoir area. (NARA)

The NKPA received some tank reinforcements from the Soviet Union in 1951 after the Chinese intervention. Also in 1951, the 105th Tank Division was reorganized as the 105th Mechanized Division, the 17th Mechanized Brigade was given divisional status, and the 10th Mechanized Division was formed though not equipped. A number of separate tank and assault gun battalions were also formed on paper. However, Soviet resupply was completely inadequate to equip these units, and in 1951 the NKPA armored force numbered only 77 T-34-85 tanks and 63 SU-76M assault guns. By 1952, the NKPA decided to drop the pretense: it disbanded the 17th and 105th Mechanized Divisions and converted the 10th Mechanized Division back to an infantry unit. The vehicles and crews on hand were used to form six separate tank/assault gun regiments. By war's end, the NKPA armor units mustered 255 T-34-85 tanks and 127 SU-76M assault guns, yet these saw little if any combat in the final years of the war.

The Chinese People's Liberation Army (PLA) had very little tank support during its intervention in 1950. At the end of the Chinese Civil War in 1949, the PLA had a force of 349 tanks, consisting mainly of Soviet-supplied Japanese Type 95 light tanks and Type 97 medium tanks, as well as smaller numbers of American M3A3 Stuart light tanks and M4A4 Sherman medium tanks captured from the Nationalist Kuomintang army during the war. These tanks were nominally organized into the 1st and 2nd Armored Divisions and two independent tank regiments.

By May 1950, the PLA tank force had been increased modestly to 410 tanks, mainly by combing the civil war battlefields for abandoned or damaged vehicles. Few of the tank units were fit for combat, so in August 1950 the existing units were consolidated into three tank brigades, with a remainder used to form tank training centers. In the meantime, the Soviet Union agreed to a major increase in arms sales, intended to support the Chinese involvement in Korea. In October 1950, ten Soviet tank regiments moved into northern China. Over the next three months, the Soviet crews instructed their Chinese counterparts on using the tanks, which were then turned over to the PLA. So, for example, two Soviet tank regiments deployed to Xuzhou, where they transferred their equipment to the 3rd and 4th Tank Regiments of the PLA's 2nd Armored Division; a similar process was undertaken with the 1st Armored Division and the two independent regiments. Each Chinese regiment received 30 T-34-85 tanks, six IS-2 heavy tanks, four ISU-122 heavy assault guns, and various items of support equipment (by 1953, the Soviet Union had sold the PLA a total of 278 T-34-85s, 38 IS-2s, 48 SU-76M light assault guns, and 27 ISU-122s).

Chinese T-34-85 tank units were first deployed to Korea in February 1951 and saw limited combat. After being decimated in the summer fighting, the PLA 3rd Tank Regiment was withdrawn to China for rebuilding and took part in the 1953 National Day Parade in Tiananmen Square in Beijing to honor its service.

In February 1951, the Chinese People's Volunteer Army (CPV) in Korea was reinforced with four tank regiments: the 1st and 2nd from the 1st Armored Division, the 3rd Tank Regiment from the 2nd Armored Division, and the 6th Separate Tank Regiment. These did not fight as unified bodies, but were usually spread out to support Chinese infantry formations. So, for example, the 3rd Tank Regiment was split between the Thirty-Ninth and Forty-Third Armies during the June 1951 fighting. It took part in 18 engagements and claimed to have knocked out two US tanks. However, the unit was almost wiped out in the process, and was withdrawn to China in the following July. It was replaced in June 1952 by the division's 4th Tank Regiment. A tank of this unit, number 215, claimed five tank kills along with numerous bunkers and other targets destroyed, and was honored as a "People's Heroic Tank" and displayed at the PLA museum in Beijing. The Chinese tank interventions in Korea were extremely small-scale, and were so minor that most US accounts assert that no Chinese tanks were encountered in the 1951–53 fighting.

The garishly marked "tiger" M46 tanks of the 6th Tank Battalion are seen here at Yangpung on March 7, 1951, while supporting the 24th Infantry Division.

ASSESSMENT

Although the North Korean armored force had substantially outnumbered its US equivalent at the beginning of the war, by August 1950 the US Army began to enjoy the numerical advantage in armor. By the end of 1950, US tank units in Korea had received 1,326 tanks, consisting of 138 M24 Chaffees, 679 M4A3E8 Shermans, 309 M26 Pershings, and 200 M46 Pattons.

A 1954 operational survey concluded that there had been 119 tank-vs.-tank actions during the war, 104 involving US Army tank units and 15 involving the 1st Marine Tank Battalion. On the US side, the tanks that were involved were the M4A3E8 in 59 actions (50 percent); M26 in 38 actions (32 percent), M46 in 12 actions (10 percent), and M24 in 10 actions (8 percent). Most of the tank battles were on a very small scale, and only 24 engagements involved more than three North Korean tanks. A total of 34 US tanks were knocked out by North Korean T-34-85 tanks or SU-76Ms, of which only 15 were totally lost; the rest were repaired and returned to action. The US tanks knocked out 97 T-34-85 tanks, and claimed a further 18 as probable. Not surprisingly the M24, with its thin armor, proved the most vulnerable to enemy tank fire. At least four M24s were knocked out by the T-34-85's 85mm gun.

Notwithstanding the M24, the T-34-85 was generally less able to resist hostile tank fire than the US tanks. It could be penetrated by the fire of any of the US medium tanks, while it had difficulty punching through the M26 or M46 armor. The M26 and M46 were indeed a clear overmatch for the T-34-85, with thicker armor and heavier firepower. The T-34-85 and the M4A3E8, however, were on fairly equal terms. Although the M4A3E8 had a gun of smaller caliber, the widespread availability of HVAP ammunition made it quite capable of penetrating the T-34-85's armor. Likewise, the T-34-85 had no particular problem penetrating the armor of the

M4A3E8 at normal combat ranges. US operational research concluded that the M26 was about three times more effective than the M4A3E8.

If the T-34-85 was penetrated, its crew was far more vulnerable to injury. A US inspection of T-34-85s found that 75 percent of the crews were killed when hit by tank fire, compared with only 18 percent in the case of US medium tanks hit by T-34 fire. This imbalance was in part due to the US tankers' practice of hitting a tank repeatedly until it burned to make certain that it was knocked out. In general, the study concluded that the T-34-85 was an excellent tank, but that the North Korean crews were not as well trained as their American opponents. The US lost 136 tanks in 1950, but the main source of loss (69 percent) was mines. In contrast, a total of 239 T-34-85 and 74 SU-76M wrecks were counted by UN intelligence in October 1950, surprisingly close to the figure of 258 T-34-85s initially supplied by the Soviet Union. A total of 296 T-34 hulks were identified as of April 1952.

In 1950, the US Air Force claimed to have destroyed 857 tanks in air attacks, several times the number actually present, and about eight times higher than actual results. Through June 1952, the Far East Air Force also claimed 1,256 tanks destroyed and 1,298 damaged; there were also 123 kill claims by Marine Corps and allied land-based aircraft, and another 163 tanks were destroyed and 161 damaged by Marine Corps and US Navy carrier-based aircraft. Of the original 239 T-34-85 wrecks surveyed by US intelligence, 102 were attributed to aircraft (60 percent of these to

After the withdrawal from the Chosin reservoir, the Marine 1st Tank Battalion remained in eastern Korea. It was assigned the task of ferreting out North Korean soldiers who had escaped northwards into the hills after the failed September Naktong offensive. Here, the crews use their .50-cal. machine guns, mounted on M26A1 and M4A3 (105) tanks, to fire on NKPA forces in the hills. (NARA)

As the Korean War went into stalemate along the 38th Parallel the role of tanks changed, and they were often used for artillery fire support. Here, some M4A3E8s from the 72nd Tank Battalion provide fire support for the 23rd Infantry, 2nd Infantry Division, north of Pia-ri on the east-central front on September 18, 1951.

napalm) and 13 to bazookas; a later assessment downgraded the confirmed air kills to only 29, though many of the unknown kills were likely due to napalm air attacks. The excessive kill claims by aircraft are similar to assessment issues in World War II. Part of the problem stemmed from aircraft repeatedly hitting the same tanks, as well as the difficulty of distinguishing tanks and trucks when making high-speed passes in poor weather conditions. The US Navy was credited with 12 tanks destroyed by naval gunfire. The table below is based on a second and larger survey of the tank wrecks.

The opinion of US tankers about the various types of US tanks changed in 1951 once the T-34-85 threat disappeared. The M26 Pershing was undoubtedly the most sought-after type in 1950, when the tank fighting was still intense. But once the tank fighting declined after 1950, the M26 was shunned due to its automotive shortcomings, particularly its sluggish performance on hills and its sloppy transmission. Those tankers with experience in the M4A3E8 preferred it over the M26, since it was more reliable, easier to maintain, and far more nimble to drive. Its automotive performance in the hilly Korean countryside was far superior to that of the M26, and its firepower was perfectly adequate against the now rarely encountered T-34-85. The M46 cured many of the problems encountered with the M26 due to the introduction of a new engine and cross-drive transmission, and so was preferred over the M26.

NKPA tank losses by cause, July–November 1950

Cause	Destroyed	Damaged	Total
M24 light tank	1		1
M26 medium tank	29	3	32
M4A3E8 medium tank	41	4	45
M46 medium tank	18	1	19
Tank sub-total	89	8	97
Artillery	20	8	28
Bazooka	11	11	22
Recoilless rifle	9	4	13
Land mine	1		1
Grenades	3		3
Aircraft	27	2	29
Unconfirmed	63		63
Total	223	33	256

Tempo of T-34-85 losses to US tanks, August–November 1950

	August	September	October	November	Total
M24				1	1
M4A3E8	2	23	20		45
M26	3	21	8		32
M46		4	5	10	19
Total	5	48	33	11	97

FURTHER READING

Not surprisingly, coverage of the Korean tank fighting is much more detailed for the American side than the North Korean side. A US operational research team attempted to catalog the experiences of captured North Korean tank unit veterans for the studies listed here. Of the 28 men located in prisoner-of-war camps, only a few were tank crewmen and most were from support or headquarters elements; none from the decimated 105th Armored Brigade. The bibliography below is focused on studies directly related to the tank fighting, though the official US Army and Marine histories were also consulted.

GOVERNMENT REPORTS

Anon., Technical Manual TM9-735, *Medium Tanks M26 and M45*, Department of the Army (August 1948)

Anon., Field Manual FM17-12, *Tank Gunnery*, Department of the Army (November 1950)

Anon., Technical Manual TM9-374, *90mm Guns M3 and M3A1 for Combat Vehicles*, Department of the Army (August 1950)

Anon., *Organization and Combat History of the North Korean 105th Armored Division*, Eighth Army G-2 (1950)

Anon., *Engineering Analysis of the Russian T34/85 Tank 1945 Production*, Chrysler Corporation Engineering Division (September 1951)

Anon., *Vseobecny popis tanku a jeho bojava a technicka charakteristika T-34-85*, Czechoslovak Defense Ministry (1956)

Coox, Alvin, *US Armor in the Anti-Tank Role: Korea 1950*, Operations Research
   Office (July 1952)
Thompson, Milton, et al., *Employment of Armor in Korea: The First Year*, Armor
   School, Ft. Knox (May 1952)
McDonald, H. W., et al., *The Employment of Armor in Korea*, Operations Research
   Office (April 1951)
McRae, Vincent and Alvin Coox, *Tank-vs.-Tank Combat in Korea*, Operations
   Research Office (September 1954)
Robertson, William, *Counterattack on the Naktong 1950* (*Leavenworth Papers No. 13*),
   US Army Combat Studies Institute (December 1985)

ARTICLES

Conner, Arthur, "The Armor Debacle in Korea 1950: Implications for Today,"
   Parameters (Summer 1992) pp.66–76
Kwang-Soo Kim, "The North Korean War Plan and the Opening Phase of the
   Korean War," *International Journal of Korean Studies* (Spring/Summer 2001)
   pp.11-33

BOOKS

Daily, Edward, *Strike Swiftly: Korea 1950–53 – 70th Heavy Tank Battalion*,
   Turner (2000)
Estes, Kenneth, *Marines Under Armor: The Marine Corps and the Armored Fighting
   Vehicle 1916–2000*, Naval Institute (2000)
Gilbert, Oscar, *Marine Corps Tank Battles in Korea*, Casemate (2003)
Kolomiets, Maksim, *T-34: Pervaya polnaya entsiklopediya*, Eksmo (2009)
Ustyantsev, Sergey and Dmitriy Kolmakov, *Boevye mashiny Uralvagonzavoda Tank
   T-34*, Media-Print (2005)
Lototskiy, S. S. (ed.), *Voyna v Koree 1950–53*, Poligon (2003)
Vanin, Yu. V. et al., *Voyna v Koree 1950–53 gg.: Vzglyad cherez 50 let*, Pervoe
   Marta (2001)
Webb, Raymond, *The 72nd Tank Battalion in Korea 1950–1952*, Toppan (1953)
Zaloga, Steven, *M26/M46 Pershing Tank 1943–1953*, New Vanguard 35,
   Osprey (2000)
Zaloga, Steven and Jim Kinnear, *T-34-85 Medium Tank 1944–1994,* New
   Vanguard 20, Osprey (1996)
Zaloga, Steven and George Balin, *Tank Warfare in Korea 1950–53*, Concord (1994)

INDEX

Figures in bold refer to illustrations